Contents

Welcome to the
Tower of London

In the early 1070s, William the Conqueror began to build a massive stone tower at the centre of his London fortress. Nothing like it had ever been seen in England before. The ruthless William intended his mighty 'White Tower' not only to dominate the skyline, but also the hearts and minds of the subjugated Londoners. He succeeded beyond his wildest dreams; nearly a thousand years later the Tower of London still holds us in its thrall.

William's mighty fortress is now a World Heritage Site that welcomes over two million visitors a year. People from all over the world come to discover the Tower's myriad stories. If you listen carefully, you may still hear the steady beat of its powerful heart, deep within the ancient stone walls ...

What to see

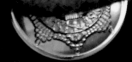

To help you make the most of your day at the Tower of London we've devised some special tours of the important buildings and exhibitions, so you don't miss anything!

Tour 1:
Making an entrance

Edward I's magnificent western entrance must have impressed visitors arriving in the 13th century. Follow in their footsteps as you pass through the Middle and Byward towers and along Water Lane. This tour also includes the notorious Traitors' Gate and Henry III's Watergate. See pages 18-21

Tour 2:
The Medieval Palace

St Thomas's Tower, the Wakefield Tower and the Lanthorn Tower are today known collectively as the 'Medieval Palace', which was once a surprisingly comfortable royal home. The rooms, including Edward I's bedchamber complete with replica medieval bed, are presented with sound and aromas to re-create life in the times of Henry III and his son Edward. See pages 24-7

Tour 3:
Imprisoned at the Tower

Some of the most famous executions in English history took place at the private scaffold site on Tower Green; here you can imagine the last moments of three Tudor queens. Discover the prisoners' graffiti in the Beauchamp Tower, torture instruments in the Lower Wakefield and a murder mystery in the Bloody Tower. See pages 32-7

The Yeoman Warders

The Yeoman Warders (often called 'Beefeaters') have been at the Tower of London since the 14th century. Join one of their famously entertaining tours and enjoy 60 minutes of intriguing stories, secrets and bloodthirsty tales of the Tower! For details of their guided tours (English only) and other free events, see the information boards marked on your map.

The Fusiliers' Museum

The Royal Regiment of Fusiliers was founded in 1685 by James II to protect the royal guns within the Tower, two of which can be seen flanking the steps of the museum. Inside you'll find many fascinating and unusual exhibits from the history of the regiment, including a copy of a large metal 'boot' used in 1808 to cure a malingerer!

The ravens

The ravens are one of the most famous sights at the Tower of London, and legend has it that if they ever leave, the kingdom and the Tower will fall! The birds all have names and very different characters; discover their stories next to their lodgings.

Special events

For details of today's special events, see the information boards – their locations are marked on your map.

Tour 4:
The Crown Jewels

This fabulous array of world famous coronation regalia is not to be missed! The Tower has been home to this priceless collection since at least the 17th century, and it has been admired by visitors ever since. You'll also enjoy the exhibition in the Martin Tower: *Crowns and Diamonds: the making of the Crown Jewels.* See pages 42-5

Tour 5:
Inside the White Tower

There are three fascinating floors to explore in this mighty building. Visit the exquisite St John's Chapel, a rare survival from the Norman period; be awed by the thrilling displays of aristocratic armour and weaponry (including some made for Henry VIII); and don't miss the block and axe in the Spanish Armoury. See pages 50-3

Tour 6:
The East Wall Walk

The huge defensive inner curtain wall, mostly built by Henry III, makes an interesting walk on the east side of the fortress, from the Salt Tower to the Martin Tower. The Lower Bowyer Tower on the North Wall Walk is also open, allowing a visit to another rare surviving medieval interior. See pages 56-9

The history of the Tower of London

'This Tower is a citadel to defend or command the city; a royal palace for assemblies or treaties; a prison of state for the most dangerous offenders; the only place of coinage for all England at this time; the armoury for warlike provision; the treasury of the ornaments and jewels of the crown; and general conserver of the most records of the king's courts of justice at Westminster.'

John Stow, *Survey of London,* 1598

The Tower of London has been all these things and more; during its long and colourful history it has changed its use and expanded in concentric rings, always with the mighty White Tower at its powerful heart. The graphic on page 14/15 will help you understand the development of the site.

The mighty White Tower at the centre of the fortress.

Right: William the Conqueror depicted on the Bayeux Tapestry.

Norman beginnings:
William and the White Tower

It is with William the Conqueror (1066-87) that the history of the Tower of London begins. In 1066, Edward the Confessor died childless, leaving several claimants vying for the throne. Edward's brother-in-law, Harold Godwinson, was crowned immediately but William, Duke of Normandy, a distant blood relative, said he too had been promised the throne.

William invaded and defeated the English under King Harold at the Battle of Hastings. Realising he must next secure England's most powerful city – London – he did not attack directly but first laid waste to the surrounding countryside. Seeing that the game was up, the city's leading men came to William to submit.

William's determination and faith in his own military might is reflected in the account of his biographer, William of Poitiers, who tells us that he sent an advance guard to London to construct a fortress and prepare for his triumphal entry into the city. After his coronation in Westminster Abbey on Christmas Day 1066, the new king withdrew to Barking in Essex, 'while several strongholds were made ready in the City to safeguard against the fickleness of the huge and fierce population, for he saw that his first task was to bring the Londoners completely to heel'.

Archaeological evidence suggests one of these strongholds was built in the south-east corner of the Roman city walls, on the site of the future Tower of London. These early defences were soon replaced with a great stone tower (the White Tower) proclaiming the physical power and prowess of the new Norman monarch.

Roman remains

Over 1,000 years earlier it was the Romans under the Emperor Claudius who were the invading force. Like their Norman successors they had been determined to impose their rule on the native inhabitants. London was their creation and the Normans were able to re-use parts of the existing Roman city walls built about AD 200 (a full height section can be seen preserved by Tower Hill underground station). The riverside location was perfect for controlling access to London, the most powerful city, and protecting against possible river borne attack.

It is not clear exactly when work started on the Conqueror's White Tower or precisely when it was finished but the first phase of building work was certainly underway in the 1070s. Gundulf, the new Bishop of Rochester, was in charge; Norman masons were employed and some of the building stone was specially imported from William's native Normandy. Labour, however, was provided by Englishmen. The *Anglo-Saxon Chronicle* comments in 1097 that 'many shires whose labour was due to London were hard pressed because of the wall that they built around the Tower'. By 1100 the White Tower was complete.

The castle as it may have looked while building the White Tower in the 1070s or 1080s.

Nothing quite like it had ever been seen in England before. The building was immense, at 36 x 32.5m (118 x 106ft) across, and on the south side where the ground is lowest, 27.5m (90ft) tall; the Tower dominated the skyline for miles around.

The Tower was protected by Roman walls on two sides, ditches to the north and west up to 7.5m (25ft) wide and 3.4m (11ft) deep and an earthwork topped by a wooden palisade.

Although many later kings and queens did spend time at the Tower, it was never a favourite royal residence. Palaces like Westminster had more opulent rooms. Equally, the Tower was not the first line of defence against invading armies, though it could rise to this challenge. The Tower's primary function was as a fortress and stronghold, a role that remained unchanged right up until the late 19th century.

The Medieval Tower:
A refuge and a base for royal power

As a power base in peacetime and a refuge in times of crisis, the Tower's fortifications were updated and expanded by medieval kings. A series of separate building campaigns ensured that by about 1350, the Tower was transformed into the formidable fortress we see today.

These building works started in the reign of Richard the Lionheart (1189-99) who, on gaining the throne, left England almost immediately on crusade. He left the Tower in the hands of his Chancellor, William Longchamp, Bishop of Ely who doubled the fortress in size with new defences.

They came just in time. In the King's absence his brother John seized the opportunity to challenge the Chancellor's authority and mount an attack. He besieged the Tower and its new defences held out, until lack of supplies forced Longchamp to surrender.

On his return in 1194 Richard regained control, John begged for forgiveness, and was later named as Richard's successor. As king, John (1199-1216) often stayed at the Tower and was probably the first king to keep lions and other exotic animals there (see page 62). His reign was characterised by political unrest; John made concessions to the barons by issuing Magna Carta in June 1215, but went back on his word as soon as he could. His opponents, who were in control of London and the Tower, invited Prince Louis of France to come and take the throne. Louis launched an invasion in 1216, but King John died suddenly in the midst of fighting for his crown.

So at the age of only 9, John's son, Henry III (1216-72), inherited a kingdom in crisis. However, within months the French were defeated at the Battle of Lincoln, and attention turned to securing the kingdom, with reinforcing the royal castles at the top of the agenda. The boy King's regents began a major extension of the royal accommodation at the Tower, including the building of two new towers on the waterfront: the Wakefield as the King's lodgings and the Lanthorn, probably intended as the Queen's.

But when rebellious barons caused Henry to seek refuge at the Tower in 1238, the nervous King soon noticed the weakness of the castle's defences. In 1238 he embarked on the building of a massive curtain wall on the north, east and western sides, reinforced by nine new towers and surrounded by a moat flooded by the Flemish engineer John Le Fossur (the ditch-digger).

This very public display of the King's power began to alarm Londoners. Contemporary writer Matthew Paris recorded their glee when a section of newly built wall and a gateway near the site of the Beauchamp Tower collapsed. Some said their guardian saint, Thomas Becket, had made a heavenly intervention. Evidence of one of the collapsed buildings was found during archaeological excavations in the 1990s.

King Edward I (1272-1307) was a more confident and aggressive leader who managed his country's rebels, but he was determined to complete the defensive works his father had begun at the Tower. Between 1275 and 1285 he spent over £21,000 on transforming the Tower into England's largest and strongest concentric castle (with one ring of defences inside another). He filled in the moat and created another curtain wall enclosing the existing wall built by his father, and also created a new moat. In spite of all this work and building comfortable royal lodgings, he seldom stayed at the Tower.

However, Edward's reign saw the Tower put to uses other than military or residential. It was already in regular use as a prison (the first prisoner being Ranulf Flambard in 1100); and Edward used the castle as a secure place for storing official papers and valuables. A major branch of the Royal Mint was established, an institution that was to play a significant part in the castle's history until the 19th century.

Edward I's less warrior-like son, Edward II (1307-27), lacking in either military skill or statesmanship, soon put the efficiency of the Tower's new defences to the test. The discontent of the barons reached a level comparable with his grandfather Henry III's reign, and Edward was often forced to seek refuge there. He took up residence in the area around the present Lanthorn Tower, and the former royal lodgings in the Wakefield Tower and St Thomas's then began to be used by courtiers and by the Wardrobe (a department which stored valuables and dealt with royal supplies).

Unlike his father, Edward III (1327-77) was a successful warrior and the captured kings of France and Scotland were held at the Tower. He carried out minor building works at the fortress and extended the wharf, before Richard II (1377-99) shepherded in another period of intense domestic strife. In 1381 the peasants revolted and 10,000 rebels under Wat Tyler burnt and plundered the capital. An unarmed but determined group managed to enter the Tower after the King had ridden out to pacify the rioters (see page 60).

King John, shown hunting in this 14th-century manuscript illumination, stayed frequently at the Tower.

Right: A groat of Edward I, the first type of coin to be struck at the Tower.

Eventually, in 1399, Richard, accused of tyranny by his cousin, Henry Bolingbroke, was forced to renounce his crown while he was held in the Tower.

Henry IV (1399-1413) was declared king the next day. His reign and that of his successor Henry V (1413-22) were quiet ones for the Tower, with very little building work or domestic unrest, but instability soon returned with Henry VI (1422-61 and 1470-1) and the Wars of the Roses.

During this struggle between the royal houses of Lancaster and York, the Tower was of key importance, and for the victorious it became a place of celebration. Henry VI held tournaments at the Tower; it saw splendid coronation celebrations for Edward IV (1461-70 and 1471-83) and victory parties for Henry VII (1485-1509), who entertained his supporters in grand style. However, for the defeated the Tower was a place of murder and execution; victims included Henry VI himself in 1471 and the young Edward V and his brother in 1483 (see below).

A scene from the Battle of Barnet, 14 April 1471, a decisive victory for Edward IV and the House of York in the Wars of the Roses.

Murder at the Tower

The disappearance and supposed murder of the two young sons of Edward IV remains one of the most intriguing stories of the Tower's history. After Edward's death in April 1483, his sons, the 12-year-old Edward V and his 9-year-old brother, Richard of Shrewsbury, were taken to the Tower on the orders of their uncle, the Duke of Gloucester. The princes were declared illegitimate in July and their uncle was crowned King Richard III. What became of the princes remains a mystery; they were never seen alive again. Rumours of their murder spread quickly and became the inspiration behind Shakespeare's villainous portrayal of Richard III.

Then in 1674, the skeletons of two boys were found hidden under a staircase leading to the Chapel of St John in the White Tower. Many people, including Charles II, considered them to be the bodies of the murdered boys, and the bones were re-buried at Westminster Abbey.

The skeletons were forensically re-examined in 1933. It was concluded that they belonged to two boys, aged about 10 and 12 years – the same age as the princes when they disappeared.

You can find out more about their story in the Bloody Tower, so named because of its traditional association with the princes' incarceration and murder. Many believe Richard III was the perpetrator – after all their disappearance undoubtedly helped him maintain his possession of the throne – but was it really that simple?

The Tudors:

The Tower as royal prison

The House of Tudor emerged triumphant under Henry VII, who added to the royal residential buildings at the Tower. Henry VIII (1509-47) continued the work begun by his father on a grander scale, erecting a large range of timber-framed lodgings, primarily for the comfort and enjoyment of his second wife, Anne Boleyn, ready for her coronation in 1533. But, they were rarely used and from this point on, the Tower ceased to be an established royal residence.

Henry VIII's decision to break with Rome swelled the Tower's population of religious and political prisoners from the 1530s onwards, while the country had to adjust itself to their monarch's new role as the Supreme Head of the new, Protestant, Church of England. Prisoners included Sir Thomas More, Bishop Fisher of Rochester and two of Henry's wives (see page 33). All four were executed.

Before his premature death, Edward VI (1547-53) continued the political executions begun by his father. Mary I (1553-8) returned the country to Catholicism and her short reign saw many rivals and key Protestant figures imprisoned at the Tower. Lady Jane Grey was executed at the Tower on the Queen's orders and Princess Elizabeth, the Queen's half-sister was imprisoned there. Elizabeth I (1558-1603) continued the trend cramming the Tower to bursting point with celebrity prisoners but, like her successor James I (1603-25), she made few improvements to the Tower's defences.

Princess Elizabeth (later Elizabeth I), was briefly imprisoned in the Tower in 1554.

Below: Sir Thomas More bids a final farewell to his daughter.

The first permanent garrison at the Tower was installed in the 17th century. This sketch shows the soldiers on parade.

The Restoration:
The Tower and the Royal Ordnance

Charles I's reign (1625-49) ushered in a long and bloody civil war (1642-9) between the King and Parliament. Once again the Tower was one of the King's most important assets. Londoners feared he would use it to dominate them but, in the end, the Tower was won by the Parliamentarians and it remained in their hands for the entire Civil War. Losing the Tower and London as a whole was a fatal blow to the King's forces and a crucial factor in Charles's defeat.

After the execution of Charles I in 1649, Parliament organised a great sale of the King's possessions. Orders were issued to take the Crown Jewels and 'cause the same to be totally broken, and that they melt down all the gold and silver, and sell the jewels to the best advantage of the Commonwealth'. Oliver Cromwell, who became Lord Protector in 1653, installed the Tower's first permanent garrison, which succeeding monarchs used to quell trouble in the city.

With the restoration of the monarchy in 1660, Charles II (1660-85) planned ambitious defences for the Tower but they were never built. The Tower's use as a state prison declined and instead it became the headquarters of the Office of Ordnance (which provided military supplies and equipment). Most of the castle was taken over with munitions stores and offices. The new Crown Jewels went on display – and in 1671 narrowly escaped being stolen (see page 45). A programme of maintenance rather than new building work characterised most of the 18th century; the existing fortifications were intermittently repaired. However, a new gateway and drawbridge were created at the east end of the outer southern curtain wall in 1774, giving access from the Outer Ward to the wharf. Efforts were made to prevent the moat silting up, with little success.

The Tower in the 19th century:
From fortress to ancient monument

Under the invigorating leadership of the Duke of Wellington, Constable of the Tower from 1826 to 1852, the moat, increasingly smelly and sluggish, was drained and converted into a dry ditch. Work on the new barracks, constructed to accommodate a thousand men – on the site of the Grand Storehouse destroyed by fire in 1841 – commenced. On 14 June 1845 the Duke laid the foundation stone on the barracks named after his greatest victory – Waterloo.

The last time the Tower exerted its traditional role of asserting the power of the state over the people of London was in response to rallies and disturbances in London in the 1840s supporting Chartist demands for electoral reform. More defences were constructed, including a huge brick and stone bastion that finally succumbed to a Second World War bomb, but the Chartist attack never materialised.

Visitor figures increased dramatically in the 19th century; now not just intrepid and privileged sightseers who were paying for a guided tour as early as the 1590s, but ordinary people enjoying a day out. It was also at the beginning of this century that many of the Tower's historic institutions departed. The Royal Mint was the first to move out of the castle in 1810, followed by the Menagerie in the 1830s, which formed the nucleus of today's London Zoo. The Office of Ordnance was next to leave in 1841 and finally, the Record Office relocated in 1858.

An increasing interest in the history and archaeology of the Tower led to a process of 're-medievalisation' in an attempt to remove the unsightly offices, storerooms, taverns, and barracks and restore the fortress to its original medieval appearance (see box).

In 1838 three of the old cages from the Menagerie were used to make a ticket office where visitors could buy refreshments and a guidebook. By the end of Queen Victoria's reign in 1901, over half a million people were visiting the Tower each year.

The Tower in the 20th and 21st century

Two World Wars saw the Tower back in use as a prison and a place of execution. Between 1914 and 1916 several spies were held and subsequently executed there, including Franz Buschmann (see page 41). The last execution at the Tower of the German Josef Jakobs took place in 1941, the same year that Hitler's Deputy Führer, Rudolf Hess, was held there briefly, one of the last state prisoners at the Tower.

During the Second World War bomb damage was considerable and a number of buildings were destroyed, including the mid-19th-century North Bastion, which was hit directly in October 1940. The moat was used for allotments and vegetable growing. The Crown Jewels were removed to a place of safety.

Today the Tower of London is one of the world's major tourist attractions and a World Heritage Site, attracting over two million visitors a year from all over the world.

The Hospital Block, which was partly destroyed by a wartime bomb in 1940.

The new 'medieval' Tower

The way the Tower looks today is largely thanks to a 19th-century fascination with England's turbulent and sometimes gruesome history. In the 1850s, the architect Anthony Salvin, a leading figure in the Gothic Revival, was commissioned to restore the fortress to a more appropriately 'medieval' style, making it more pleasing to the Victorian eye – and imagination.

Salvin first transformed the Beauchamp Tower, refacing the exterior walls and replacing windows, doorways and battlements. Further commissions included restoring the Salt Tower (completed 1858) and making alterations to the Chapel of St John in the White Tower in 1864. Salvin also restored the Wakefield Tower, so that it could house the Crown Jewels, which remained there until 1967. In the drive to complete the perfect 'medieval' castle, his successor, John Taylor, controversially destroyed important original buildings to create uninterrupted views of the White Tower and to build a new southern inner curtain wall on the site of the old medieval palace.

How the Tower developed

The Tower of London was begun in the reign of William the Conqueror (1066-87) and remained little changed for over a century. Then, between 1190 and 1285, the White Tower was encircled by two towered curtain walls and a great moat. The only important enlargement of the Tower after that time was the major extension to the wharf, begun by Edward III (1327-77) and completed under Richard II (1377-99).

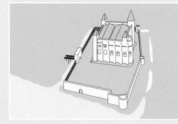

1. The Tower c1100

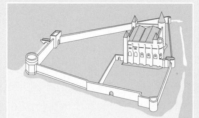

2. The Tower c1200

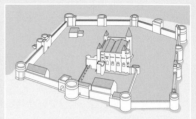

3. The Tower c1270

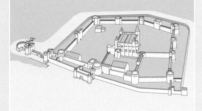

4. The Tower c1300

5. The Tower c1547

To this day the medieval defences are essentially unchanged, except for the draining of the moat.

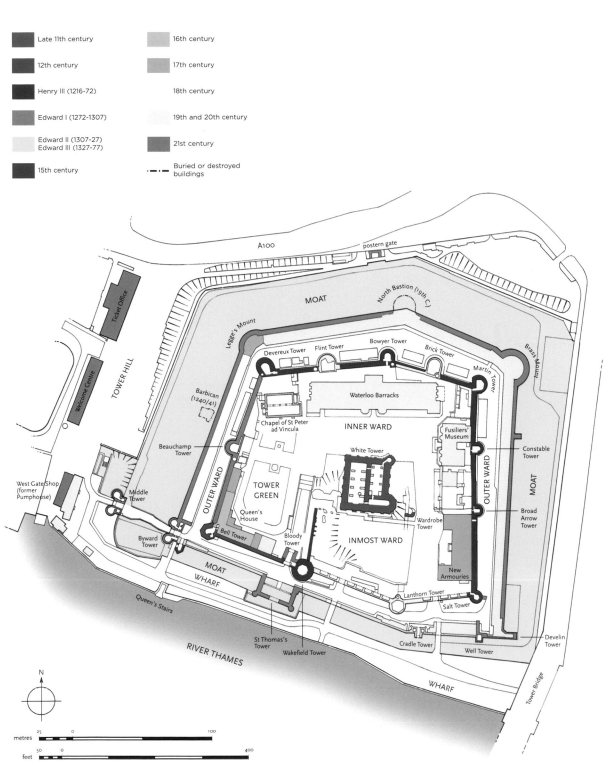

Late 11th century

12th century

Henry III (1216-72)

Edward I (1272-1307)

Edward II (1307-27)
Edward III (1327-77)

15th century

16th century

17th century

18th century

19th and 20th century

21st century

Buried or destroyed
buildings

A100

postern gate

MOAT

North Bastion (19th C)

Legge's Mount

Brass Mount

Devereux Tower

Flint Tower

Bowyer Tower

Brick Tower

Martin Tower

Barbican
(1240/41)

Waterloo Barracks

INNER WARD

Fusiliers'
Museum

Chapel of St Peter
ad Vincula

Constable
Tower

Beauchamp
Tower

OUTER WARD

White Tower

TOWER
GREEN

OUTER WARD

MOAT

West Gate Shop
(former
Pumphouse)

Middle
Tower

Queen's
House

INMOST WARD

Broad
Arrow
Tower

Byward
Tower

Bell Tower

Bloody
Tower

Wardrobe
Tower

MOAT

WHARF

New
Armouries

Queen's Stairs

Lanthorn Tower

Salt Tower

St Thomas's
Tower

Cradle Tower

Well Tower

Develin
Tower

RIVER THAMES

Wakefield Tower

WHARF

Tower Bridge

Ticket Office

Welcome Centre

TOWER HILL

N

metres   25   0   100

feet   50   0   400

15

Phil Wilson, 56, is a Yeoman Sarjeant Warder at the Tower of London. He's a member of a team of 34 men and one woman: the Chief Yeoman Warder, his second in command the Yeoman Gaoler, five Yeoman Sarjeants and 28 Yeoman Warders. Yeoman Warders need to have at least 22 years' military service; to have reached the rank of warrant officer; to have been awarded the long service and good conduct medal and to be between 40 and 55 years old on appointment.

Phil and his wife Ann, a civil servant, live in a flat in the Beauchamp Tower, which overlooks Tower Green. Phil served with the Coldstream Guards and has been at the Tower since 1997, as he tells Sarah Kilby.

Life in the day of a
Yeoman Warder

'The first sounds I hear when I wake up are the ravens croaking as they are released from their pens. It's like being on the set of a Hammer House of Horror movie!'

'I always take Ann a cup of tea in bed, as I have done for the 34 years we've been married. Then I chose which uniform to wear; I've got a whole box room full. For normal duty we wear the blue 'undress' uniform, which comes in four weights ranging from winter to super lightweight for summer.

This was developed for everyday wear around 1856, when it was discovered air pollution after the Industrial Revolution was causing the expensive red dress uniforms to rot. We now only wear it on ceremonial occasions. It's heavy, but not uncomfortable, and costs around £6,000 so you have to be careful not to spill anything on it should you happen to be eating, which is difficult as you can't see your plate over the Tudor ruff!

The 35 Yeoman Warders work shifts to cover different duties, which include the duty of watchman (who originally would literally 'watch' the gate all night), looking after visitor safety and conducting the guided tours. We're outside most of the time and it's a punishing schedule, especially during a long hot summer. You've got to be fit. Because I'm a Yeoman Sarjeant I have management duties, so I spend some time in the office too.

Yeoman Sarjeant Wilson at your service!

It's just like a little village here; we have our church, and the village green – ok, so it once had a private scaffold on it – children live in the Casemates and you can hear them playing after school. We have a 'squire' – the Resident Governor who lives in the 'big' house – the Queen's House, and our own pub – the Yeoman Warders' club. And like any other little village, there's always someone not talking to someone else!

I enjoy doing my guided tours; I've always enjoyed history and learnt a lot since I came here. Each Yeoman Warder does their own research and develops their personal style with a mentor for three or four months. Then you have to 'perform' for the Resident Governor and the Chief Yeoman Warder and if they are happy you are let loose on the public.

About five or six times a month I take part in the ancient Ceremony of the Keys – the official 'locking up' of the Tower which has been carried out every night for over seven hundred years. My role is to turn the massive key in the outer door, and push the bolt home; it makes a most satisfying 'clunk'. Then we have the historic exchange, you can hear the words echoing down Water Lane as they have done for centuries, with only the name of the monarch changing.

The sentry cries out **"Halt, who comes there?"** The Yeoman Warder replies **"The keys."** **"Whose keys?"** **"Queen Elizabeth's keys."** **"Pass then, all's well."** Then we hand the key to the Resident Governor and the Chief Yeoman Warder says **"God Praise Queen Elizabeth"**. We all lift our bonnets and reply **"Amen"**. Then the Last Post sounds into the silence, and the ceremony is over for another night.

Friends say they have seen ghosts in our flat, but after nine hours out in the fresh air I never have problems sleeping. I certainly don't worry about being burgled! But if I wake in the night I go to the window and look down on the execution site. I always hope that I might see *something* … but I never do.'

17

Tour 1:
Making an
entrance

A look at how monarchs, their important visitors and their rather less fortunate 'guests' arrived at the Tower: Edward I's magnificent western entrance, the Middle and Byward towers, Water Lane, the Bell Tower, Traitors' Gate and Henry III's Watergate.

Today's visitors enter the Tower of London by the same route as those who came riding over the drawbridges from the late 13th century onwards. Not all the features still exist, but enough survives to be able to reconstruct the past as you enter the fortress.

The 13th-century view from Tower Hill must have been magnificent: the stone Tower rising high over the surrounding wooden buildings, and the new outer curtain wall built by Edward I (1272-1307) reflected in the water-filled moat, which protected the three landward sides of the castle.

The western entrance was built between 1275 and 1281 and consisted of three causeways and two drawbridges, a barbican (outer defence) which was later called the Lion Tower (now lost) and two twin-towered gatehouses, the Middle and the Byward towers, which survive today. The whole of this complex was surrounded by a water-filled extension of the moat.

Visitors to the Tower would have crossed part of the moat on the first of the causeways and via a drawbridge to the Lion Tower. The moat was drained in 1845 on the Duke of Wellington's orders but you can still see the Lion Tower drawbridge pit, excavated in the 1930s.

The Lion Tower took its name from the beasts kept there as part of the royal Menagerie, founded in the Middle Ages and disbanded in 1834. You can read more about the Menagerie on page 62.

You can read more about the Menagerie on page 62.

Main picture opposite: The Byward Tower today; originally approached through a complex system of outer defences and below, with the moat flooded, c1826.

The lions' dens of 1779 in the now-lost Lion Tower. Fearsome roars greeted visitors arriving at the Tower from the 14th century onwards.

The Middle Tower

If the intrepid visitor had made it successfully over the first drawbridge, a second causeway and drawbridge would have taken them to the fortified gatehouse, now known as the Middle Tower. Although the shape of the Middle Tower is 13th century, it was refaced in 1717, and the arms of George I now adorn the archway. The gate tower was once protected by arrow loops and archers, and had two portcullis gates. You can still see the grooves for these in the passageway. The building is now used as offices by the Royal Armouries.

The Byward Tower

A final causeway leads towards the mightiest of Edward I's gate towers, the Byward Tower. The Byward Tower entrance passage is protected by two immense 13th-century cylindrical turrets, bristling with arrow loops. The northern turret also sports a series of gun loops, reflecting developments in weaponry and defensive techniques.

Should any attacker manage to dodge the hail of arrows (and later, bullets) and get this far, they would have still had to breach the two portcullis gates. One gate still survives and can be seen overhead, as can the 'murder holes', intended to allow soldiers to douse fires lit by intruders (or some say for pouring boiling oil on their heads!). A groove for the second portcullis shows where it used to be. Safely through the passageway, Water Lane beckons.

Water Lane, built on land reclaimed from the river.

Water Lane

Edward I achieved a major feat of engineering in 1275-85, and reclaimed Water Lane from the River Thames. Building on hundreds of wooden piles, he pushed back the river and created the Outer Ward encircled by a new outer curtain wall. On the left is Mint Street where, until 1810, the coinage of the realm was manufactured, and where Yeoman Warders and their families now live.

A very different sight would have greeted Princess Elizabeth, later Elizabeth I, in 1554 when she arrived at the Tower on the eve of her imprisonment on 18 March. It is likely that she came through the Byward Postern, opposite the end of Mint Street. The fine vaulting and carved lion's head on the ceiling of the gateway indicate that this point of arrival at the Tower was important – a sort of discreet entrance for prestigious 'guests'. The postern is protected by a wedge-shaped turret, fitted out with state-of-the-art gun loops.

The Bell Tower

This ancient polygonal Bell Tower, originally lapped by the water of the Thames, is the second oldest tower in the fortress after the White Tower. Built in the 12th century, probably for Richard the Lionheart, the Bell Tower is so called because the curfew bell has rung from it for at least five hundred years, although the current bell dates from 1651.

The tower was protected from undermining by its faceted shape, and defended by arrow loops. As it adjoined the home of the chief Tower official it was extremely secure and was considered very suitable for important prisoners. Sir Thomas More and Bishop John Fisher were committed here in 1534 for refusing to swear allegiance to Henry VIII as Supreme Head of the Church of England.

Part of the plinth at the base of the Bell Tower is exposed, showing how tall it was before the Outer Ward was built around it in the next century. The huge inner curtain wall connecting the Bell Tower to the Bloody Tower was also built in the late 12th century. It now forms the back wall of the Resident Governor's house.

The notorious Traitors' Gate.

Thomas Cranmer, Archbishop of Canterbury, who was imprisoned at the Tower for high treason in 1556, shown arriving at Traitors' Gate.

Traitors' Gate

This is the most notorious of all the Tower's entrances. It's not hard to imagine the dread of those ill-fated prisoners such as Sir Thomas More and Anne Boleyn, accused of treason, arriving here at the Tower. However, not all the history of this most grand of entrances is so grim. Originally built for Edward I between 1275 and 1279, this new watergate called St Thomas's Tower was a daring variation on the traditional defensive gate tower. Discreetly defended by arrowloops, the building had gilded window bars and painted sculpture on its exterior. Edward's royal barge could be moored beneath the great archway, built using cutting edge Crusader castle-construction technology gleaned from the King's time fighting in the Holy Land.

The timber framing above the archway is a memento of happy times for Anne Boleyn. It was constructed in 1532 by Henry VIII's Master Carpenter, James Nedeham, as part of the excited rush to renovate the Tower ready for Anne's coronation in June 1533.

Henry III's Watergate

The Bloody Tower gateway is a reminder of the old position of the Thames. It was built in the early 1220s as Henry III's river entrance, protected by arrowloops and soldiers stationed in the lower chamber of the Wakefield Tower next to it. As king, Henry had a small private entrance on the other side of the Wakefield Tower, which allowed him to arrive discreetly and go straight up to his royal apartments above. Traces of a staircase can still be seen. Around 1280, when the foreshore was infilled to create the Outer Ward, the gate became a land entrance into the Inner Ward. The gateway was extended and developed by subsequent kings and later became known as the Bloody Tower. The elaborate vaulting in the passageway dates from Edward III's reign (1327-77) and proclaims that this entrance was one of status and dignity. The portcullis gate can be glimpsed overhead as you pass through to the Inner Ward.

Beauty of the Byward

Golden lions, lilies and pretty parakeets – the interior of the Byward Tower reminds us that the Tower of London has not only been a grim fortress prison. Sadly, this intriguing room is too fragile to open to public view, explains Curator Jane Spooner.

The harsh reputation of the Tower can sometimes conceal a richer and subtler history. Medieval castles were not used purely as military buildings. As a royal fortress, it was important that some of the Tower's interiors should be decorated luxuriously, in keeping with the owner's status.

Tantalising hints of how the Tower must have once looked are revealed in the fragments of ancient wall paintings that survive in Edward I's Byward Tower. Hidden away on the first floor lurks a riot of gold and green ... the most surprising secret of the Tower of London.

During renovations in 1953, a great ceiling beam, decorated with lions 'passant guardant' (walking past and looking at you), 'popinjays' (parakeets) and 'fleurs-de-lis' (lilies), was discovered. Further investigations ensued, and medieval and Tudor wall paintings were uncovered.

The room's decoration is enigmatic, but enough survives to piece together some clues.

The green and gold background of the wall and beam paintings resembles 14th-century Italian textile designs, and includes symbols from English royal heraldry. The lions are traditionally English, but ever since the 1340s the fleurs-de-lis of France have also been incorporated in English royal heraldry as Edward III had claimed the throne of France. These symbols are enclosed within a popinjay pattern.

The figures on the wall are St John the Baptist, the Virgin Mary, St John the Evangelist and St Michael the Archangel weighing souls. The mourning Virgin and the praying Evangelist suggest that the most important image in between them, now lost, was of Christ on the Cross. The faces and angel's wings are painted with rare delicacy, and the use of expensive pigments and gold leaf indicate that the work was of the highest quality and probably by artists commissioned at the end of Richard II's reign. John the Baptist was Richard's patron saint, and appears in other commissions associated with the King.

Why was this room decorated with such exquisite paintings? There is very little evidence of what the room was used for – but there are suggestions that it could have once been a chapel, or was used for weighing coins in the Exchequer, or as part of the nearby Constable's lodgings.

The paintings are a unique survival, although the Tower was once decorated with many more. For example, accounts tell us that Henry III had a room painted with the story of Antioch – a chivalric tale of crusading knights. His queen's chamber was painted with flowers and red lines simulating mortar joints between stones.

The medieval painting would have been considered old fashioned in later centuries and was probably covered over by the time the chimneybreast and fireplace were inserted. The 16th-century red and white rose painting on the chimneybreast declared the allegiance of the Tower to a new and powerful dynasty – the Tudors.

Medieval wall paintings are very fragile, and sadly this tiny room in the Byward Tower is not robust enough to withstand huge numbers of visitors. Some pigments are light sensitive and the painting has suffered from earlier and less-informed conservation treatments. Our conservators now monitor the room's environmental conditions and we hope that information gathered will help us preserve this most precious and surprising of interiors for future generations to enjoy.

The paintings are a unique survival, although the Tower was once decorated with many more.

Tour 2:
The Medieval Palace

Here are lodgings fit for a king, surprisingly comfortable and presented to give a glimpse of life during the reigns of medieval monarchs Henry III and his son Edward I.

St Thomas's Tower, the Wakefield Tower and the Lanthorn Tower are today known collectively as the 'Medieval Palace'. They lay at the heart of what was formerly the residential area of the Tower, richly decorated and comfortable lodgings grand enough for any medieval monarch. Built by Henry III (1216-72) and his son Edward I (1272-1307), they have been re-presented for today's visitor to evoke a vivid picture of 13th-century life, complete with sounds and smells.

Medieval monarchs never stayed at the Tower for very long, and it was usually for a specific purpose rather than pleasure, although the palace had to be fit for royalty, even for short visits. Edward I, for example, only stayed here for 53 days in 35 years of rule.

St Thomas's Tower

St Thomas's Tower was built by Edward I between 1275 and 1279. The first room – which records describe as a 'hall with a chamber' – has been left unrestored. This was where the King dined and entertained.

Many people have lived in St Thomas's Tower since Edward's day, and the archaeological evidence has been preserved. Remains of the hall's huge 13th-century fireplace, the corner of a garderobe (toilet) wall and a picturesque vaulted turret can still be found. The wharf which now separates St Thomas's Tower from the Thames had not been built in the 13th century, and Edward's building would have looked out directly on to the river. Its impressive façade would have declared to river travellers the magnificence of this warrior king.

A short film explores the very different characters of Henry III and Edward I, and explains how each used the Tower. Edward mostly stayed to supervise building work and prepare for war, whereas his more timorous father sought shelter behind its strong walls from rebellious barons. Both kings extended the Tower's defences considerably (see page 15).

Edward I's bedchamber has been re-created to show the style in which he might have stayed in November 1294, when we know that he was briefly at the Tower, checking on his fortress and getting ready for war. A combination of 13th-century records, manuscript illuminations, objects and antiquarian drawings were used to build up what we believe is an accurate picture.

Edward I's oratory; the little 'chapel over the water'.

The bedchamber is reconstructed using replicas based on original 13th-century furnishings and archaeology. The room shows the King's bed, close to the fireplace for warmth, but allowing him a view of the little oratory, the 'chapel over the water' mentioned in records. The wall paintings are based on the floral 'pointing' described in accounts for Edward's mother at the Tower.

Because the court moved around the country so frequently, all the furnishings were of a type that could easily be transported, as part of the King's travelling wardrobe. The textiles are woven with designs based on the royal arms of England, and of Edward's first wife, Eleanor of Castile. To further re-create the intimacy of the rooms, sounds of conversation from the hall next door and the crackling of the fire can be heard, while Latin prayer in the oratory reminds us that this was a room for the King's private worship. The 13th-century basin for washing the vessels for Mass still survives. As king, Edward would have had fine, painted furniture, but on occasion he may have conducted private business in the room, and eaten on a small simple table attended by only his closest associates.

From St Thomas's Tower a covered bridge, built in the 19th century on the site of an earlier one, leads to Henry III's Wakefield Tower.

A comfortable home for kings: the Medieval Palace.

Above: Henry VI, imprisoned during the Wars of the Roses, was supposedly murdered while at prayer in the Wakefield Tower in 1471.

Left: The Crown Jewels display in the Wakefield Tower was a magnet for visitors.

The Wakefield Tower

The Wakefield Tower was built as part of Henry III's lodgings between 1220 and 1240. As it was then set at the river's edge, Henry would have been able to enter this room from his private stairs and postern gate.

This was probably a private audience chamber – the elaborate architecture and small chapel reflect Henry's piety and attention to artistic detail.

A short film describes how the King used the Tower to protect himself from, and also to defeat, his enemies.

The vaulted ceiling is a 19th-century reconstruction. The fireplace and chapel have recently been restored – the screen is a copy of one very like that described in a detailed order by Henry '... and for making a good and suitable screen of wooden boards between the chamber and chapel of the new turret facing the Thames ... 16 pounds, 3 shillings and 8 pence'.

By Edward I's death in 1307, the Wakefield Tower had been abandoned as a residence, and was used for the storage of official documents. Subsequent kings' private chambers were relocated to the Lanthorn Tower. From 1870 until 1967 the Crown Jewels were displayed here.

Henry VI

By tradition the chapel in the Wakefield Tower is linked to the death of Henry VI (1422-61 and 1470-1), who was imprisoned at the Tower in 1471 by the Yorkist Edward IV. This was during the Wars of the Roses, when two branches of the royal Plantagenet dynasty (Lancastrians and Yorkists) fought for the throne. Henry was reputedly lodged in the Wakefield Tower and murdered while at prayer. A small plaque in the chapel floor commemorates this unfortunate event.

The Wall Walk:
The lost palace

The Wall Walk is 19th century and its construction destroyed the remains of the rest of Henry III's lodgings. In the 13th century, the Medieval Palace consisted of much more than St Thomas's and the Wakefield towers. The enclosed area in front of the White Tower is called the Inmost Ward. In the 13th century it was a busy complex, full of buildings set up to serve royal residence. These included kitchens and a great hall. The Inmost Ward was protected by the Main Guard wall (which still survives behind the ravens' cages) and the enormous Coldharbour Gate. Its foundations are to the left of the White Tower.

The Lanthorn Tower

The Lanthorn Tower, built as part of Henry III's queen's lodgings, was gutted by fire in 1774. The present building is 19th century. Inside, a selection of 13th-century objects illustrate the lifestyle of Henry and Edward's courts.

Edward I's son Edward II (1307-27) preferred to stay in this side of the castle when in residence at the Tower, and the Lanthorn Tower was eventually adapted into the king's chambers.

The Tower of London was a home as well as a castle; Henry III and Edward I would both have stayed here with their families. Children lived within the Tower in the 13th century as they do now. The Lanthorn Tower today displays a range of objects that help tell the story of life in the Medieval Palace, from a beautiful and rare rock crystal chesspiece, to this rather battered pewter toy knight.

How the Medieval Palace might have looked in c1300, on the completion of works by Edward I.

Life indoors in the Middle Ages

Ex-Python and medieval historian Terry Jones on the very public, fast-changing and probably rather jolly medieval way of life.

I am convinced that human beings don't change through the centuries. The people who were seizing, wielding and exercising power in 500 BC were very similar to those who were doing the same in AD 2000. And the people, like you and me, who allow them to get away with it, are also pretty much the same. However, that doesn't mean that the places they and we live in don't change. We only have to look at interiors of houses at the beginning of the 20th century, with their walls crowded with hanging pictures, and furniture covered with lace to see how quickly things can change. And in the Middle Ages the interiors of palaces and grand houses changed just as quickly – in fact in some ways even more quickly – because the great houses of the Middle Ages were usually in a state of constant flux.

As we walk around the Medieval Palace at the Tower of London we should try not to imagine the rooms as static entities. For a start, rooms were often multi-functional – they could have different uses throughout the day, and the furniture would change and be rearranged to accommodate those requirements. Tables, for example, were usually set up on trestles when they were needed, and then taken down again when the meal was over. Indeed a permanent table (table dormant in Middle English) was such a rarity in Chaucer's day (late 14th century) that he comments on the fact that one of his characters (The Franklyn) possesses such a luxury!

His table dormant in his hall always
Stood ready covered all the long day.
The Canterbury Tales, 1353-4

'Comfort' for someone in the Middle Ages was more about feeling that you were in the right space.

Previous page: A great lord dining in the 15th century. Medieval rooms were multi-functional; tables would be dismantled once dinner was over and furniture rearranged as needed.

Above: A re-created interior in the Medieval Palace today.

So rooms could change throughout the day more than we would expect them to do today. They might also change according to who was using them, because interiors would be expected to reflect the importance and pecking order of whoever happened to be in them at the time. But there was even more fluidity to castle and palace interiors. This was because the great households would be constantly on the move. The kings, in particular, lived itinerant lives, moving from one court to the next, one palace to the next, one castle to the next.

Whether this was the result of the pressure such a large household (with all its hundreds of servants and courtiers) would place on the local community, or whether it was a question of moving on once the sanitation arrangements showed signs of strain, I don't know. Perhaps it was just that the king and his great lords needed to make their presence felt in the various parts of the country over which they had lordship. Perhaps they just enjoyed the change of scene. But move around the country they certainly did. And wherever they went – more often than not – they took their furniture

with them. So for much of the year these great halls and chambers would probably have been pretty empty – more like we see them today – awaiting the arrival of the great men.

By the 15th century, this itinerancy had more or less come to a halt, and life would have been more settled. But in the years when the Medieval Palace here at the Tower was in use, the court would have been constantly coming and going throughout the year.

Another thing we should bear in mind as we move through these spaces is that they would have been crowded. In the Middle Ages life was lived in public. The concept of privacy as we would understand it didn't enter into how people lived until perhaps the 17th century. Medieval rooms, particularly the large rooms known as halls, had to accommodate everyone: lords and ladies, children, servants, friends, visitors, guests, officials, petitioners, hangers-on and so forth. In the same room some people would have been doing business, some would have been playing games, some might have been cooking, some might have been entertaining themselves. I suppose we should think of life in the medieval hall as being a little more like a market place or maybe a continual party!

But this all meant that the perception of interior space was different from the way we perceive it today. In modern times we tend to see walls as things that keep some people out and which provide us with intimate space – privacy. But in the medieval house, walls were all-inclusive and embraced everyone at once. This must have meant that one's whole perception of interior space was different: for example, where you were in the room would have been important and what you were sitting on would have had significance. A chair was more a statement about who was sitting on it, than a thing designed for comfort. In fact even knights and important men might find themselves sitting on stools or benches, while only the king, perhaps, sat on a chair.

The point is that 'comfort' for someone in the Middle Ages wouldn't have meant having a back to your chair, or a soft carpet under your feet – it was more about feeling that you were in the right space, in your correct place in the pecking order. No one would have felt 'comfortable' sitting on the king's seat or in the great lord's place at table. And we shouldn't despise the people of the Middle Ages for this. The idea that 'comfort' is entirely to do with shutting out the cold or protecting the body from hard surfaces is no more a universal definition of the word than using it to define social roles and positions. Tastes and fashions and even the concepts behind them do change – even though human beings themselves are fundamentally unchanging.

The people of the Middle Ages were not simpler or less intelligent or less capable than we are today, but their goals and social organisation were different, and this found expression in the way they designed their houses and the way they furnished them. And when we walk round these rooms and halls of the Medieval Palace here at the Tower of London, we are glimpsing the lives of the folk of the Middle Ages, through the lens of architecture and interior design. We are looking at ourselves but in a different world.

We should think of life in the medieval hall as being more like a continual party!

This 13th-century manuscript is the only surviving picture of Edward I in a medieval interior and provides evidence of the richness of the decoration.

Tour 3:
Imprisoned at the Tower

The Tower of London is soaked with the bloody history of England's dynastic and foreign wars. Hundreds have entered this place, only to leave for a miserable march to a place of execution outside the Tower.

Tower Green

Ten people were beheaded on this peaceful greensward that stretches to the west of the White Tower. Three of these were English queens.

Anne Boleyn, the second wife of Henry VIII, was in her early 30s; Catherine Howard, Henry's fifth wife, barely in her 20s: both had been accused of adultery; neither may have been guilty. Lady Jane Grey, queen for nine days, was only 16, the innocent pawn in a failed military coup by her father, the Duke of Northumberland.

Social convention ensured that right up until the end they were treated in the manner befitting their status. 'Shall I go into a dungeon?' Anne had asked on her arrival at the Tower. 'No, madam', came the reply, 'You shall go into the lodging you lay in at your coronation.' The irony was keenly felt. Anne would kneel down and weep 'in the same sorrow' and fall 'into a great laughing'. On the day of her execution, she enquired, 'I heard say the executioner was very good, and I have a little neck.' She was executed by a clean stroke of an expert swordsman specially imported from France.

Walk in the footsteps of those condemned to death on Tower Green and reflect at the execution site with its thought-provoking memorial. Pause in the ancient Chapel Royal of St Peter ad Vincula, discover the prisoners' graffiti in the Beauchamp Tower and see the instruments of torture in the Lower Wakefield Tower, before finding out the truth concealed in the Bloody Tower.

The actual site for all three of these executions was different – with a special scaffold and block being prepared each time – but all took place within a few yards of each other, close to where the present execution site memorial is now positioned. This memorial also recalls the death of the seven other men and women to die on or near this spot.

Those remembered are Jane Boleyn, Viscountess Rochford (and erstwhile sister-in-law to Anne Boleyn) who died alongside Catherine Howard. As her lady-in-waiting, she was complicit in the Queen's alleged adultery. Margaret Pole, the 70-year-old Countess of Salisbury, was executed by Henry VIII for her supposed involvement in a Catholic invasion. A blundering executioner 'hacked her head and shoulders to pieces'. Robert Devereux, Earl of Essex, was also executed away from public gaze, on the orders of Elizabeth I. The authorities supplied two axes to ensure the job was done properly.

These royally directed executions were committed within the bloody century of Tudor rule, between 1536 and 1601. They are book-ended by the deaths of four more men, whose guilt was also thoroughly questionable. William, Lord Hastings, was beheaded in 1483 probably on the orders of Richard of Gloucester, who was in the process of a messy takeover of the throne. He would become the infamous King Richard III. In 1743, Farquhar Shaw and the cousins Samuel and Malcolm Macpherson were shot at dawn on Tower Green in front of their regiment, the 'Black Watch', for being ringleaders in a so-called mutiny.

Gentle visitor pause awhile • where you stand death cut away the light of many days • here jewelled names were broken from the vivid thread of life • may they rest in peace while we walk the generations around their strife and courage • under these restless skies

Brian Catling, creator of the execution site memorial

The Chapel Royal of St Peter ad Vincula.

The Chapel Royal

Three English queens and Rochford, Salisbury and Essex are all buried in the Chapel Royal of St Peter ad Vincula (above). They share their burial place with other famous prisoners of the Tower, including two saints of the Roman Catholic Church, Thomas More and John Fisher (both executed on Tower Hill). Their graves are overshadowed by memorials to many of the Tower officials responsible for the safe incarceration of prisoners. The Chapel still operates as a place of worship for the 150 or so people that live within the walls of the Tower today.

But the history of imprisonment at the Tower is a much longer story than this account of Tower Green suggests. The first prisoner arrived at the Tower on Wednesday 15 August 1100. Ranulf Flambard had been Bishop of Durham and chief tax-gatherer for William II. Under the new king, Henry I, he was accused of extortion and hauled off to the White Tower in chains. Over eight hundred years later, on

15 August 1941, Josef Jakobs was executed by firing squad at the Tower, guilty of spying for Germany during the Second World War. In between, the Tower was home to kings and queens, priests and heretics, Welsh, Scottish, French, German and American prisoners of war, thieves and politicians, terrorists and soldiers, aristocrats and prostitutes.

Richard II was imprisoned in the Tower then deposed in 1399.

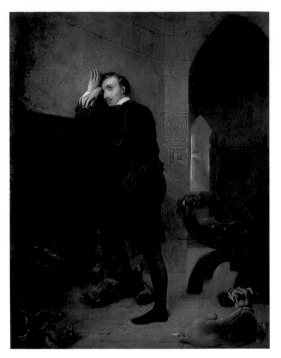

Above: Prisoners' graffiti in the Beauchamp Tower, carved mainly between 1532 and 1672.

Right: Philip Howard, Earl of Arundel (1557-95) was imprisoned in the Tower in 1584 by Elizabeth I for being a Catholic. Expecting execution daily, he eventually died of infection ten years later.

The Beauchamp Tower

The Tower was not constructed as a prison, and there were no purpose-built cells. Prisoners were squeezed in anywhere. The Beauchamp Tower to the west of Tower Green is part of the inner defensive wall built by Henry III and Edward I around the White Tower. But the tower takes its name from Thomas Beauchamp, Earl of Warwick, who was imprisoned there at the end of the 14th century. The Beauchamp Tower has been used to house prisoners, off and on, throughout its history, and its walls are swathed in the graffiti they left behind.

The vast majority of inscriptions date from the 16th and 17th centuries, when political and religious instability combined to establish the Tower as the foremost state prison in the country. Many of those accused of treason were guilty of nothing more than ending up on the losing side of one of the country's bitter and entertainingly complex dynastic wars. The spoils of victory were plentiful; the risks of defeat manifest. The acutely tetchy Tudors were particularly keen to keep rivals to the throne locked up.

Of course, there were genuine causes of concern. The Tudor dynasty's claim to power was notoriously weak, and bringing the Reformation to England didn't help stability. Being Protestant or Catholic became not only a statement of conscience but also frequently a declaration of political allegiance. There were plots to replace Mary I with Elizabeth I, and plots to replace Elizabeth I with practically any suitable Catholic alternative. Philip Howard, Earl of Arundel, was imprisoned in the Beauchamp Tower for ten years by Elizabeth, for no other obvious reason than being the leading Catholic peer in the country.

Under Elizabeth I, it was illegal simply to be a Roman Catholic priest in England; many were arrested and charged with treason. Some found safety in exile, others died traitors' deaths: hanged, drawn and quartered. If you were really lucky, you may even have been interrogated and tortured before your execution.

The Lower Wakefield Tower

The Lower Wakefield Tower provides a short account of the history of torture at the Tower. Only a tiny fraction of prisoners held at the Tower were tortured. Torture was essentially part of a carefully designed programme of interrogation, and only used to elicit information or to persuade the prisoner to sign a written statement to be used in law. It was, nonetheless, barbaric, and – perhaps more importantly to the authorities who abandoned its use in the 17th century – often unreliable.

The Bloody Tower

The Tower has, nonetheless, acquired a reputation as a ruthless executor of state power. It is almost as if the very stones have developed a taste for murder. The Bloody Tower of popular imagination is a good example of this. From as long ago as the early 1600s, this was because it was believed to be the place where the 'Princes in the Tower' had been murdered by their uncle, Richard III. However, there is nothing in any of the accounts that identifies the Bloody Tower

Torturer's tool, the Scavenger's Daughter, which compressed the body in a kneeling position.

as the scene for the supposed murder. The identification of an actual site responds in part to a need in all of us to find a focus, a sense of 'history where it happened' which previous Tower authorities have been more than happy to satisfy. (See page 10 for more evidence on the Princes.)

The more prosaic truth of this particular tower is that it was originally called the Garden Tower and was a secure 'home' for many years to Sir Walter Ralegh where, although a prisoner, he was often visited by his family. Ralegh wrote his unfinished *History of the World* here and conducted scientific experiments in the gardens.

Imprisonment at the Tower of London has in this way always varied from the luxurious to the lethal. Some certainly enjoyed particularly comfortable 'imprisonments'. King John the Good of France enjoyed a royal diet, and the company of a section of his court, including an organist and 'Master John the Fool'. But for many others, the reality of imprisonment was grim indeed: real physical torture, mental anguish and the threat of a trial or summary execution.

Eventually, the Tower's infamy and popularity as a visitor attraction outgrew its usefulness as a prison. The days of being locked up for your religious views, or on the tyrannical whim of a paranoid ruler, are – thankfully – over. Aren't they?

High status prisoners enjoyed many luxuries, as this reconstruction of Sir Walter Ralegh's room shows.

Prisoners in love

Passion (and prudent jailers) sometimes triumphed over circumstance; many high status prisoners were allowed visits from partners and lovers, and at least one baby was conceived in captivity, as novelist and screenwriter Philippa Gregory reveals.

When we think of prisoners held in the Tower we conjure up images of dripping dungeons and solitary days of terror, but for some prisoners life could be quite comfortable. Those who were of high status on entry or – if their luck changed – might be people of power and influence on their release, could command all sorts of benefits.

The warders of the Tower were well aware that today's prisoner charged with treason against one monarch, might tomorrow be the loyal supporter and friend of a newly triumphant royal rival. This delicate situation was even more acute when warders were expected to guard a claimant to the throne. Sudden death in those dangerous days might mean that the traitor-heir was suddenly the legitimate king or queen. An astute jailer would try very hard to avoid complaints of bad treatment.

This was a very vivid difficulty in the case of Princess Elizabeth who was brought to the Tower in March 1544 under suspicion of conspiring with a rebellion against her sister Mary Tudor, Queen of England.

Elizabeth arrived by river, brought discreetly by barge so that the Londoners should not see her and riot in her defence. She had delayed her departure as long as she could hoping to miss the tide, and when she arrived she dropped down to sit in the rain, and refused to go in. But when her ladies-in-waiting started to cry for her she bounced up in irritation and went to her four rooms in the royal palace.

How were the jailers to treat her? If her half-sister died, Elizabeth, then aged 21, would be the next queen of England, and everyone wanted to avoid potential offence. So she was allowed to walk in the gardens, knowing full well that her childhood playmate and great love of her life Robert Dudley (1532-88) was imprisoned nearby, probably in the Beauchamp Tower.

Robert was held for his share in the plot to put his sister-in-law, the Protestant claimant Jane Grey, on the throne. Though there are well-loved romantic tales that the young queen-to-be and her friend met in secret it is most unlikely that this happened. The closest that they could have come would have been to walk on the narrow flat roof between one prison and another; but they would have taken that exercise alone.

But it does seem probable that their shared time of imprisonment was one of the many bonds that held them together through a life-long affection. Princess Elizabeth's mother, Anne Boleyn, died on Tower Green, and Robert saw the execution of his father on Tower Hill. The two young people understood very well the danger as well as the opportunities of the Tudor world.

Robert Dudley was visited by his wife Amy Robsart in the Tower. His brother, Guildford Dudley, was husband to the doomed Lady Jane Grey, who had been declared queen for only nine days, and was then imprisoned by

Above: Lord Nithsdale's wife helped him escape from the Tower, disguised as a woman, in 1716.

Main picture opposite: Actors Joseph Fiennes and Cate Blanchett as fellow Tower inmates Robert Dudley and Princess Elizabeth in the 1998 film *Elizabeth*.

Mary Tudor. Guildford too asked to see his wife Jane before his death. However, though she wrote to him that she forgave him and his father for the plot that had destroyed them all, she would not see either of them.

Tower legend has it that Guildford Dudley carved the 'Jane' graffito (below) that still survives on the stone walls of the room where the Dudley brothers were imprisoned in the Beauchamp Tower.

Jane's sister, Catherine Grey (1540-68) was imprisoned later under Queen Elizabeth, for the offence of making a secret marriage to Edward Seymour without the Queen's

permission. Her marriage was discovered when she had to admit that she was pregnant. As the grand-daughter of Henry VIII's sister, Catherine did have a claim on the throne. Elizabeth, angry and fearful of the birth of another potential heir, had the young couple imprisoned.

Catherine's first baby – that rare thing, a Tudor boy – was born and baptised in the Tower. Sympathetic jailers let her husband into her room and the young couple managed to conceive a second child in the Tower.

Elizabeth's anger at this news was intense, and merciless. The furious Queen kept husband and wife apart, but released both to separate house arrest because of plague raging in London. Catherine died five years later of tuberculosis, never having been reunited with the man she loved. Edward went on to marry twice more, and both children survived to adulthood. Catherine and Edward's grandson, William Seymour, features in another story of thwarted love at the Tower.

Lady Jane Grey encountering the corpse of her husband Guildford Dudley as it is returned from the scaffold.

'Is it really true he will never come back to me?'

Among the records at the Tower is a copy of a moving letter from the bewildered and grief-stricken wife of Franz Buschmann, a businessman arrested for spying in London during the First World War. Born in Paris, of a naturalised Brazilian father and Danish mother, his German-sounding name and business dealings attracted suspicion. He was convicted, and sentenced to death. Buschmann spent his last night at the Tower, and was allowed to play his beloved violin through the night as a comfort. When the guard arrived in the morning, he is said to have kissed the violin, saying 'goodbye, I shall not want you any more'.

He was executed at the Tower by firing squad on 19 October 1915.

The East Casemates Rifle Range, c1915, where Buschmann was executed.

The marriage of heirs to the throne was a constant worry to the reigning monarch. The marriage of William Seymour to Arbella Stuart in 1610 was regarded as a threat by the new King James I. As the King's cousin, it was illegal for Arbella to marry without royal permission.

Arbella was imprisoned under house arrest at Lambeth, but her husband was sent to the Tower. A spirited and rebellious girl, Arbella escaped from her prison disguised as a man, and formed a plot with William's barber to smuggle him out of the Tower in a cart. His escape was successful but he missed their rendezvous and poor Arbella had to set sail for France alone. News of her escape preceded her and her ship was captured, and Arbella returned to imprisonment, this time in the Tower. William managed to cross the Channel safely and found freedom in France, but he never saw Arbella again. She died at the Tower in what is now the Queen's House in 1615. Arbella seems to have lost her will to live, and her reason toward the end,

and appears to have starved herself to death. There are many reports of her heartbroken ghost returning to haunt the Queen's House.

The Jacobite rebellions brought a new crop of prisoners to the Tower. In 1716 William, Earl of Nithsdale, was imprisoned for his part in supporting the exiled Stuart king. He was allowed a visit by his wife, the courageous Winifred Maxwell. She brought women's clothes for him and disguised him as one of her ladies-in-waiting. By keeping up loud and distracting conversation, and with ladies rushing in and out of the cell, they managed to confuse the guards. All the 'ladies' finally got past a rather dazed guard, who remained unaware that Nithsdale had gone. Nithsdale and his wife escaped successfully to the Continent.

Tour 4:
The Crown Jewels

No visit to the Tower is complete without seeing this breathtaking, world famous collection of fabulous finery in the Waterloo Barracks. Don't miss the exhibition on the making of the Crown Jewels in the Martin Tower, too.

An avenging Hercules adorns the handle of the 1735 Christening Ewer, used for the christening of George III in 1738.

The Supertunica, made in 1911 and the Imperial Mantle, 1821.

St Edward's Crown, 1661.

'Yes, these are the real ones' is the answer to the most frequently asked question of the Jewel House Wardens. Visitors are sometimes surprised to learn that the real gems are not hidden away in a secret vault; that they are able to stand a few centimetres away and gaze on the most valuable collection of crowns, coronation regalia and jewels in the world.

The Crown Jewels look the part. They are gloriously ornate, intricately made and have inspired acts of greed, violence and even spawned stories of evil curses. They also stand as a potent symbol of Britain's enduring monarchy.

Most of the gold and silver jewel-encrusted pieces on display in the Jewel House are those objects used at the coronation of a sovereign and are collectively known as the Coronation Regalia. The coronation is about recognition, anointing and investiture and for this reason the regalia includes swords of state and ceremonial maces, carried in procession before the sovereign, as well as orbs and sceptres, trumpets and tunics. There is even a Coronation Spoon, used for anointing the sovereign with holy oil.

Other items in the collection include historic pieces no longer used at coronations, and items used in the Coronation Banquet (which no longer takes place). The collection has been added to at various points, and in the 17th century was almost completely replaced after its destruction during the Commonwealth.

Having done away with the monarchy, Parliament sought to do away with the royal regalia as well. The crowns were 'totally broken and defaced' and the plate was sent to the Mint to be melted down into coinage. The remaining items were sold.

After the restoration of the monarchy in 1660, Charles II ordered a splendid new set of jewels. Sir Robert Vyner, the King's goldsmith, needed three tons of silver to restock the Jewel House. The most modern objects on view today were made for the 1953 coronation of Queen Elizabeth II.

The Queen Consort's Ivory Rod with Dove, 1685, Queen Mary II's Sceptre with Dove, 1689 and the Queen Consort's Sceptre with Cross, 1685.

The Sovereign's Orb, 1661 (detail).

The Crown Jewels have been at the Tower of London since at least the 17th century in various locations. They first went on public display in the Martin Tower when, astonishingly, visitors were allowed to touch the jewels after handing a small donation to the Jewel House Keeper! It seems hardly surprising then, that the Crown Jewels were nearly stolen in 1671 (see box). The dashing and impudent Irishman 'Colonel' Blood carried out an almost-successful raid on the Jewel House, having knocked the Keeper on the head with a mallet and smashing down the arches of the State Crown so as to hide it under his cloak.

The visitor today will soon realise that security has been stepped up a little since the 17th century. The Crown Jewels are now housed in the Waterloo Barracks, built in the 19th century on the site of the Grand Storehouse, which was destroyed by fire in 1841. The Barracks were originally built to provide accommodation for almost a thousand soldiers. The soldiers are still here (although there are not so many) and security for the Crown Jewels still rests with an ex-soldier, the Resident Governor of the Tower.

Much of the collection is in fact silver-gilt (solid silver covered with a thin layer of gold), though there are plenty of solid gold objects too. Look out for St Edward's Staff, made of gold with a steel spike at its end, and the gold and enamelled Armills, also known, rather splendidly, as the bracelets of sincerity and wisdom.

Other pieces that date from the 17th century include the Sovereign's Sceptre with Cross and the Sovereign's Orb. The orb represents worldly power; the cross on top symbolising Christian rule. The orb and sceptre made for Charles II have been used at every coronation since – including the coronation of Queen Elizabeth II.

Our current monarch was crowned with St Edward's Crown, also made in 1661, but modelled on the lost medieval crown of English kings, named after King Edward the Confessor (1042-66). Tradition has it that gold, melted down from the original crown, was used in its construction. On leaving the ceremony, Queen Elizabeth received the lighter Imperial State Crown in its place. It is this crown which The Queen wears every year at the State Opening of Parliament.

The Stuart Sapphire at the back of the Imperial State Crown, 1937.

The Crown Jewels incorporate some spectacular precious stones. Until the reign of George IV (1820-30), jewels were usually hired, placed in their settings for the coronation, and then returned after the event. The crown frames were then reset with pastes for display in the Jewel House. George IV tried to insist that the jewels for his coronation crown should be purchased and permanently set. This has more consistently been the case since the early 20th century, helped by the discovery of enormous, priceless diamonds in parts of what was the British Empire.

These stones include Cullinan I (the First Star of Africa) set in the Sovereign's Sceptre with Cross. This is the largest top quality cut diamond in the world, weighing just over 530 carats. The Koh-i-noor diamond from India is set in the Crown of Queen Elizabeth The Queen Mother. The stones in the Imperial State Crown include the legendary 'Stuart Sapphire', the 'Black Prince's Ruby' and 'Queen Elizabeth's Pearls'. This last crown has 2,868 diamonds, 17 sapphires, 11 emeralds, 5 rubies and 273 pearls.

There are four pieces of the older pre-Civil War set of regalia that still survive. Three ceremonial swords probably date from the reign of Charles I (1625-49), while the 12th-century silver-gilt Coronation Spoon was returned to the Tower by a Royalist sympathiser who had bought it at a sale in 1649. The spoon is used for anointing the sovereign during a coronation, using holy oil poured from a gold Ampulla, in the form of an eagle.

There is an exhibition about the making of the Crown Jewels in the Martin Tower.

More detailed information about the Crown Jewels can be found in The Crown Jewels: Official Guidebook *available in the Tower shops or from our website* **www.hrp.org.uk**

'Stop thief!'

Early in the morning of 9 May 1671, Thomas Blood arrived at the Tower of London with three companions: his son Thomas, Robert Perot and a thug called Richard Halliwell. All were secretly armed with knives, pocket pistols and swordsticks. They tied up Talbot Edwards, the Keeper of the Crown Jewels, and gagged him by ramming a piece of wood in his mouth. The old man was told that if he remained quiet he would come to no harm but he struggled so much that he was stabbed and given 'several unkind knocks on the head'. With Edwards immobilised, the three men helped themselves to the treasures in front of them. Just as Blood and his accomplices prepared to make their way out of the Tower, fate intervened in the form of Talbot Edwards's son. Having been abroad for several years, he returned home unexpectedly and raised the alarm. The gang members tried to make their escape but, after a brief scuffle in which shots were fired, they were overpowered and captured.

Blood was an intriguing and complex character. He was a reckless, violent adventurer, who had seen some military service, but his rank of 'Colonel' was purely of his own invention. Exactly why he wanted to steal the Crown Jewels is not clear. His motives may just have been mercenary. Some say it was simply for the thrill of it. Whatever his reasons, rather remarkably, Charles II pardoned him.

The crown is down!

The day the State Crown fell to the floor, and other magnificent mishaps, revealed by Clare Murphy.

Despite the immense value and highly symbolic nature of the Crown Jewels, they have not been immune from the odd disaster ...

👑 Queen Victoria was not amused when her Imperial State Crown was badly damaged at the State Opening of Parliament in 1845. Pity the poor Duke of Argyll, who while proudly carrying the crown on a cushion let it fall to the ground with a 'great crash'. The Queen later described it as 'all crushed, & squashed, looking like a pudding that had sat down'.

👑 Queen Mary II's Sceptre with Dove was made for the joint coronation of William III and Mary II in 1689 and was not used again. In the late 18th century, someone tidily put it away ... and forgot all about it. Fifty years later this splendid sceptre was discovered 'at the back part of a shelf ... enveloped in dust'.

👑 William IV's big day was ruined by a severe toothache at his coronation in 1831. The pain was made far worse by the weight of his State Crown (over 3.2kg/7lbs) pressing down on his head.

👑 Queen Victoria must have been gritting her teeth when the Coronation Ring had to be forced on to her finger by the Archbishop of Canterbury during the coronation ceremony in 1838. It had been incorrectly made to fit her little finger instead of the adjoining one and was consequently much too small. The Queen later recorded in her diary: 'I had the greatest difficulty to take it off again – which I at last did with great pain'.

👑 The Imperial State Crown was carried on top of George V's coffin to his lying in state in Westminster Hall in January 1936. During the procession, a sudden jolt caused the topmost cross to fall to the ground. The late king's son and heir, Edward VIII, witnessed the incident and later remarked, 'It seemed a strange thing to happen; and, although not superstitious, I wondered whether it was a bad omen.' A few months later Edward VIII abdicated ...

The Sovereign's Sceptre with Cross has been used at every coronation since 1660 but does seem to have suffered more than its share of wear and tear. At James II's coronation banquet in 1685, it was badly damaged – possibly having rolled off a table – and two jewelled pieces were later found lying on the floor in Westminster Hall. (Thankfully the cleaners hadn't been in!) The sceptre was again damaged at George IV's coronation banquet in 1821 and had to be repaired after the event.

While George III was wearing his Imperial State Crown during his coronation ceremony in 1761, a large diamond fell to the ground and 'was not found again without some trouble'.

It was red faces all round in 1909, when a visiting Keeper of Metalwork at the Victoria & Albert Museum spotted that four of the St George's Salts were displayed upside down! For most of the previous century, the dragon-head brackets around the salt wells had been mistaken for feet! The error was discreetly rectified, and he of course promised not to tell a soul, well maybe one or two close friends ...

And finally, it's reassuring to know that monarchs are as nervous as the rest of us before big occasions. George VI was convinced that the Archbishop of Canterbury would not be able to distinguish between the front and the back of St Edward's Crown. So to avoid embarrassment, he had a piece of red cotton tied to the front of it before the coronation ceremony in 1937. Unfortunately, the cotton was removed before the event and yes, you've guessed it, the King was crowned back to front!

The mighty White Tower

In 1075 Londoners could only stand and stare as the White Tower rose up to dominate their skyline. You can still feel that same sense of awe today, observes Edward Impey, former Curator of Historic Royal Palaces.

The White Tower is not only among the best preserved and the most interesting 11th-century buildings in Europe but, since its creation by William the Conqueror, has been a potent symbol of authority and nationhood. Begun in 1075-9, building was continued by William Rufus (1087-1100) and was probably finished by 1100, when his chief minister, Ranulf Flambard, was imprisoned in it by Henry I. Flambard's celebrated escape, by befuddling his guards with wine and climbing down a rope hidden in the barrel, was the first in the Tower's history.

The new building had three main functions. Firstly, it was itself a fortress, probably considered impregnable at the time of its construction. Secondly, its vast interiors must have been designed for the king's occasional use and as the setting for major governmental and ceremonial functions. But its third purpose, and the one that required it to be a tower, was perhaps the most important – to serve as a permanent reminder to the new Norman nobility and the native population of the king's authority.

Even today it dominates the castle, but its impact when built, looming over the early Norman city and its riverborne approaches, must have been extraordinarily powerful. Although the first in England, the White Tower was not, however, the first building of its type, for since at least the 10th century the kings and great nobles of northern France had been building 'keeps' or 'great towers'. Moreover, it now seems that important features of the White Tower's layout may have been borrowed from a particular building in Normandy of about AD 1000. Its building, however, contributed enormously to the development of the 'great tower' as a type, providing a prototype for dozens more in Britain and France.

As built, the White Tower contained two floors above a deep basement, each with two vast rooms and, in the case of the upper one, a chapel. Above this there is now another floor, but recent discoveries have shown that this was inserted only in the 15th century, replacing the original roof that had been surrounded by (rather than resting on top of), the upper parts of the walls. The precise purpose of the four main rooms is unknown, but they were probably intended for successively grander and more private functions as their distance from the entrance increased.

Although, as it happened, such functions were soon taken on by other buildings in the bailey below, limited ceremonial use continued throughout the Middle Ages, as did its embellishment: most importantly, in March 1240 Henry III had the building coated in whitewash, soon adding lead downpipes to protect it from water falling from the roof.

But from the 14th until the 19th century, the main use of the White Tower was as a military storehouse, and it was adapted accordingly. From this function, however, emerged the role it serves today, as a museum of arms and armour, the first visitors being admitted by at least the 1590s, and the first displays deliberately created for them in 1807. Meanwhile, its continued usefulness and symbolic importance ensured that its external appearance was not neglected, the elegant turret roofs being added in the 1530s, and the windows enlarged and given new surrounds in 1637-8, under the ultimate direction of Inigo Jones. Further works to the windows and other masonry details and stonework in the next two centuries, and the removal of the last of the attached buildings in the 1880s, left the White Tower looking much as it does today.

Edward Impey is Director of Research and Standards at English Heritage.

The White Tower as depicted in about 1480, showing scenes of the imprisonment and release of Charles, Duke of Orléans, captured at Agincourt in 1415.

Tour 5:
Inside the
White Tower

Today, the interior of the White Tower offers two main things for the visitor to enjoy: the building itself and a magnificent selection of items belonging to the Royal Armouries, the museum of the Tower of London. England's national museum of arms and armour since 1985, the Royal Armouries is an institutional descendant of the various bodies that managed the nation's munitions from the Middle Ages to the mid-19th century. Since these operated from the Tower of London and used the White Tower, the displays also tell their story and that of the storage and exhibition of weaponry here over five hundred years.

For reasons of security and dignity the only doorway to the White Tower, as built, was well above ground level and must have been reached, as now, by an external stair. The entranceway itself, complete with barrel-vault, arched seats for sentries and arrangements for barring the door, was similarly designed both for security and as a suitably impressive introduction to what lay beyond.

The entrance floor

The first room, the largest on the entrance floor, is now dominated by a full-size reconstruction of the Tower's celebrated 17th-century display of small arms, together with a model of the magnificent Grand Storehouse which housed them. Beyond lies the vaulted room below

St John's Chapel, now telling the story of the so-called 'Spanish Armoury' of the 1660s, a miscellany of objects with which the Spaniards were supposedly preparing to defeat and torture the English at the time of the Armada. Next, in the smaller of the two main rooms, stands the 'Line of Kings', a partial re-creation of another propaganda exercise, first recorded at the Tower in 1660, comprising mounted and armoured figures of English sovereigns.

The first floor

The route then leads, via a 17th-century stair, to St John's Chapel on the floor above. This is not only the best-preserved and the most attractive interior in the building, but is also one of the most complete examples of early Anglo-Norman ecclesiastical architecture in England. In form, thanks to the aisle (separated off by its twelve massive columns), the arcaded gallery above and the barrel-vaulted central space, it resembles the east end of a much larger church. And although the castle later had another chapel, it was St John's, at the heart of the royal and ceremonial apartments of the White Tower, which remained the more important: the wide arch in the west wall (to the left on entry) may have framed a throne intended for the king himself. But as with the rest of the White Tower, from the 14th century the chapel was used largely for storage and in the 1320s it was put to use as a repository for records, a function it served until 1858.

The block and axe have been displayed together since the middle of the 19th century. The axe, possibly Tudor, was once labelled dramatically – but incorrectly – as the axe used to behead Anne Boleyn (she died by sword). The block is traditionally believed to be the one used at the last public beheading on Tower Hill – that of Lord Lovat in 1747.

A remarkable roof

A glance overhead in the top rooms of the White Tower reveals one of the building's remarkable but least-known features – its gigantic roofs, constructed in 1490, early in the reign of Henry VII. Unlike most wooden roofs of anything like this span, their strength comes not from a series of complicated triangular trusses, but from single load-bearing beams stretching from wall to wall. Those over the larger room, at 13.1m (43ft), in places over 70cm (2ft) thick and weighing 3.5 tonnes (3.44 tons), are the largest ever used in England. The skill, effort and determination involved in finding the trees, shaping the timbers, carrying them to London and above all hoisting them over 30.5m (100ft) into the air and manoeuvring them in place, adds up to a staggering engineering achievement.

The next room is the eastern and smaller of the two main rooms at this level. Since at least the late 15th century this has been overlain by the inserted floor above, and obstructed, since

at least 1603, by wooden posts to reinforce it. Originally, however, it was covered directly by the roof, which, open to the rafters, would have given it a much loftier and grander appearance. To the right can be seen one of the building's four original wall fireplaces, among the very earliest in England, and from which the smoke escaped through holes in the walls rather than a proper chimney. In the far corners are original garderobes housed within the wall-thickness. Exhibits include material on the building's history and a model of the castle as it might have looked in 1547.

The next room, originally also open to the roof, would have been the most impressive in the building and among the most impressive in England at that time. As such, it probably served in a sense as a great hall, used for large scale royal ceremonies and receptions. It too was equipped with a fireplace (not visible). Put to many uses over the centuries, it now contains an array of royal and aristocratic armours and weaponry of the 16th and 17th centuries, including equipment made for

Henry VIII and others at the Greenwich workshop that he founded in 1514. Some of this material was in the White Tower and being shown to visitors as early as 1597.

The second floor

The route then leads, via an original spiral stair, to the building's top floor, inserted in 1490. Straight ahead is a stretch of the barrel-vaulted gallery that runs round most of the building at this level and which originally looked inwards on to the roof-slopes: drains that carried rainwater from the roof to gargoyles on the outside have recently been found under its floor. The wall on the opposite side of the room, pierced by a series of arches, was originally in the open air and carried a north-south walkway, at battlement level, across the building.

The displays here illustrate the Tower of London's history in the design, manufacture and issuing of munitions, and include replicas of the gunpowder racks that once filled large parts of the White Tower. On the far (south) wall of the room beyond, used for exhibitions, can be seen a giant triangular soot stain, a legacy of the smoky fireplace below and important evidence of the place and form of the original roof.

The basement

Descending the great spiral stair, linking all floors of the building, leads to the basement, dominated by the massive brick vaulting of 1737 and housing a display of 17th and 18th–century artillery. Beyond this is a small vaulted room, its rounded east end determined by the form of the chapel two floors above: the door, a remarkable survival, was made for this position in about 1350. The room contains a number of 19th-century models, clearly showing the extent of the castle's transformation in that period. On the way out, through the western half of the basement and the shop, note the well, dug during the initial building of the White Tower.

Armour for agility

This Japanese armour of c1610 is a souvenir of the very earliest years of English contact with Japan. It was one of two armours entrusted in 1613 to the merchant John Saris as diplomatic gifts to James I by the Shogun, Tokugawa Hidetada (in power 1605-23). It was on display at the Tower by at least the late 17th century, although misleadingly presented as the 'armour of the Great Mogul', ruler of India. In contrast to European armour, designed for maximum protection at the expense of mobility, the Japanese equivalent offered less protection but allowed the agile weapon-handling that was the special skill of the knightly samurai class (and their superiors) for whom it was made. As such it was composed of strips of metal and rawhide, lacquered for decoration and against rust, held together and embellished with silk braid, and crowned – as in this case – with an elaborate and fearsome helmet.

A knight in shining armour

This fabulous silvered and engraved armour was made for a young, slender Henry VIII in c1510-15. Thom Richardson FSA, Keeper of Armour and Oriental Collections at the Royal Armouries, takes a closer look.

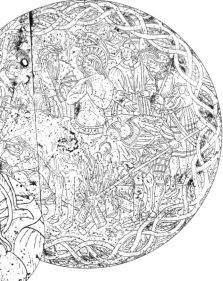

Engraved decoration on the bard showing the martyrdom of St George.

This is the earliest of the six surviving armours of Henry VIII, made for him when he was still slim and cut a dashing figure on horseback! It was made as field armour for the King by either a Flemish armourer working in Flanders or by a Flemish or Italian armourer in Henry's service at Greenwich. It weighs 30.13kg (66.5lb), which is not particularly heavy; it's roughly what modern infantry carry into battle on foot.

The horse armour, or bard, was made by a Flemish armourer, Guille Margot, in Brussels. The armour was brought to the Tower between 1644 and 1649, and has been displayed there ever since except when out on temporary loan. The decoration is the work of Paul van Vrelant of Brussels, who held the appointment of Henry's 'harness gilder' from 1514 until at least 1520. The steel armour is engraved, silvered and originally gilt with an elaborate design illustrating the two patron saints of Henry and his wife Katherine of Aragon: St George on the left hand side and St Barbara on the right, together with their heraldic badges, the rose and the pomegranate. The armour has a skirt or 'base' fashionable in the early 16th century, decorated on its border with applied letters H and K joined by true lovers' knots, most probably celebrating the marriage of Henry and Katherine in 1509.

1. On the left side of the crupper (rump defence) are three violent scenes from the life of St George. At the front he is tortured in a bull-shaped cauldron of molten lead, but is protected by the Lord. At the rear the saint is tortured on two wheels fitted with swords, but is undamaged by them. The upper panel shows his execution.

2. On the right side of the crupper St Barbara is driven through a gateway by her father, Dioscorus, at the front. At the rear of the crupper she is escorted by men with bundles of twigs for whipping. On the upper panel she is executed by her father for refusing to recant her Christianity, and in the same scene, her father is shown dead after being struck by lightning. At the rear of the crupper the initials H and K, with a rose, are supported by putti (cherubs).

3. The lower border of the bard is decorated with the King's motto *Dieu et mon droit* (God and my right), interspersed with roses and pomegranates.

The mark of the armour maker, possibly Peter Fevers, on the back of the armet.

6. The helmet – called an **armet** because it encloses the head fully – has a pivoted visor and is made with large cheek pieces that hinged to the skull to allow the King to put it on. It is decorated all over entwined with foliage flowering with rose blossoms and fruiting with pomegranates. The 'Tudor' red and white rose was one of Henry VIII's badges and the pomegranate one of Katherine of Aragon's.

7. On the left boss (domed section) of the **peytral** (designed to protect the horse's chest), St George is brought before the procurator Dacian and refuses to recant his Christianity. On the right side St Barbara talks to masons about building a third window, representing the trinity, into a tower they are constructing. At the front of the peytral you can see St George slaying the dragon.

8. The **curirass**, or breastplate, is decorated with a figure of St George fighting the dragon. The saint is depicted in armour of the early 16th century, though the historical St George was a Roman soldier said to have been executed in the reign of the Emperor Diocletian in AD 303. The backplate is decorated with a figure of St Barbara with the tower in which she was imprisoned.

4. The plate **sabatons** (foot defences) of the armour are decorated on the toes with the portcullis badge of Henry VIII and the castle badge of Castile for Katherine of Aragon.

5. The side panels or flanchards are decorated with winged mermen holding shields with combined rose and pomegranate badges, flanked by portcullis and sheaf of arrows badges for the King and his queen.

9. The knee defences (**poleyns**) are decorated with the sheaf of arrows badge of Katherine of Aragon's father, Ferdinand II of Castile, and the combined rose and pomegranate badge of the Queen.

Tour 6:
The East Wall Walk

Starting from the Salt Tower in the Inner Ward, explore the massive defensive inner curtain wall and the four towers: the Salt, the Broad Arrow, the Constable and the Martin Tower, once home to the Crown Jewels.

This huge stone encirclement, defended by eight mural towers, was part of Henry III's refortification of the castle in the mid-13th century. Four of these towers are open to the public, on the east side of the wall.

Henry's reign was tumultuous and he needed the Tower to be strong for his own protection, and to present an impression of strength to his enemies. In 1238 Henry fled to the Tower to escape the hostile reaction to the secret marriage of his sister to Simon de Montfort. The Tower's defences were clearly out of date, and Henry set about remedying the situation. Between 1238 and 1241 over £5,000 was spent on building the curtain wall and towers, a great gateway and on digging a moat. By 1285 these had been surrounded by Edward I's Outer Ward, outer curtain wall and a rather more successful moat (see page 15). You can see these later additions from the Wall Walk.

The inner curtain wall transformed the defences of the Tower. Archers and missile-throwing machines along the walls, and within the mural towers, had a good command of the land around the castle and could concentrate projectiles against an attack at any point. If the enemy managed to get on to or over the wall they were exposed to missiles from the mural towers and the White Tower.

Castles also needed accommodation. The mural towers all contained two or three floors, with a sizeable chamber on each. High-ranking guests could stay in them, or important prisoners were allotted suitable lodgings with their servants.

Main picture:
A Yeoman Warder gazes out from the East Wall Walk.

Above:
Reconstruction of the Tower in about 1241, showing Henry III's enlargement of the castle and the construction of the new defensive wall to the east.

The Salt Tower

This tower originally overlooked the Thames, and in times of trouble archers on the ground floor were able to protect it by shooting through the five arrow loops. During peaceful times the room was a storehouse.

The staircase from the ground floor passes a little room and a doorway that may have led out to the 16th-century Queen's Gallery, now long gone.

The first floor chamber also has defensive arrow loops but the original 13th-century chimney hood, and a large decorative window give a sense of a more luxurious space. The heat from the fireplace would have kept Edward I's prisoner, the deposed Scottish King John Baliol, warm in the three years he was lodged here (1296-9). The convenient garderobe (toilet) upstairs is an added touch of comparative luxury.

From the Salt Tower the Wall Walk continues to the Broad Arrow Tower. The view is of the 17th-century brick New Armouries building but in the 13th century inhabitants would have gazed down on the Privy Gardens.

The Broad Arrow Tower

This tower is named after the 'broad arrow' symbol, which was stamped on goods to demonstrate royal ownership. From the 14th century, the Broad Arrow Tower was connected to the government department responsible for royal supplies – the Wardrobe. From Henry VIII's reign it was linked to the nearby Wardrobe Tower by a long storehouse, now demolished. As part of the Great Wardrobe, royal robes and valuable furnishings were kept here.

Next to the fireplace is an inscription by Giovanni Battista Castiglione, Princess Elizabeth's Italian tutor. He was imprisoned here by Mary I in 1556 during Protestant uprisings that sought to place Elizabeth on the throne. Another important prisoner held in the Broad Arrow Tower was Sir Everard Digby, one of the infamous Gunpowder Plot conspirators who had attempted to blow up Parliament in 1605.

Walking along the next stretch of the Wall Walk, it's possible to catch a glimpse of life behind the scenes at the Tower. Yeoman Warders and their families live in the old Hospital Block to the left, and down in the Outer Ward in the 19th-century 'Casemates' – attractive cottages built in a medieval style.

The Constable Tower

The 19th-century Constable Tower is built on the site of one of Henry III's mural towers. It contains a model of how the Tower would have looked once Edward I had expanded his father's defences, by about 1300.

The Martin Tower

This part of the Tower has strong links with the Crown Jewels. These days the jewels are kept in the Waterloo Barracks, but from 1669 until 1841, they were kept in the Martin Tower. Its brick exterior is a unique reminder of the fortress's appearance before the restorations of the 19th century.

Today, this tower houses the *Crowns and Diamonds* exhibition, which tells the story of English royal crowns, and some of their most famous stones. The Jewel House Shop is on the ground floor.

During the two hundred years when this tower was known as the Jewel Tower, the Keeper of the Regalia and his family lived in the upper storeys, and the jewels were displayed on the ground floor. The brick buildings adjoining the Martin Tower house a passageway which once connected the family home to the Outer Ward.

The first Keeper of the Regalia was the unfortunate Talbot Edwards who was coshed and bound during Colonel Blood's attempt to steal the Crown Jewels in 1671 (see page 45). Poor Edwards died three years later and was buried in the cemetery of the Chapel Royal of St Peter ad Vincula, where his memorial stone is now set into the wall.

After leaving the Martin Tower, you can visit the ground floor of the Bowyer Tower on the adjacent North Wall Walk. It is one of the few surviving medieval interiors in the mostly 19th-century northern inner curtain wall. Legend has it that George, Duke of Clarence, brother of Edward IV, was 'executed' here in 1478 by being drowned in a butt of malmsey (Madeira wine), after being arrested for treason.

A welcoming home in the Martin Tower for the Jewel House Keeper, c1840 (the Crown Jewels were kept downstairs).

The peasants are revolting!

Despite all its massive fortifications, the Tower has not always been impregnable, as Curator Jane Spooner describes.

Astonishing scenes were played out in the royal apartments at the Tower of London in June 1381, when four hundred rebels stormed the fortress during the Peasants' Revolt. This poorly-armed bunch didn't use sophisticated siege weaponry to breach this massive fortress – they simply ran through the gates, which had been left open!

William the Conqueror's White Tower and the huge curtain walls and towers of Henry III and Edward I cast a shadow of impregnable royal strength over London. But in reality, the Tower's fortunes as a defensive castle were somewhat mixed. Despite the strength of the fortifications, success depended rather more upon the loyalty and efficiency of its garrison, and the stocking of its weapon stores and food larders.

> ‘[The rebels] arrogantly lay and sat and joked on the King's bed, whilst several asked the king's mother to kiss them’.

Jean Froissart

So when the Tower 'fell' in June 1381, it fell not to a well-organised army of knights, archers and engineers with siege engines, but to a force of lower-class rebels.

The Peasants' Revolt was sparked by a new tax that everyone over the age of 14 had to pay, and it was the third in four years.

The rebellion began in the south east of England and quickly gathered momentum. A ten thousand-strong force made up of yeomen, skilled craftsmen and labourers marched on London to demand the heads of those they blamed for the tax. Oddly, they didn't blame the King, Richard II, for their suffering, and even professed loyalty to him while calling for the death of the 'traitors' who governed on his behalf.

The 14-year-old Richard, his mother and royal household fled to the Tower as the rebels plundered and burnt the capital for two days. Eventually, the fortress came within the rebels' sights. Jean Froissart, a contemporary writer, described in his *Chronicles* what happened next ...

> The king had ridden out to meet the rebels at Mile End. The Tower's drawbridges and portcullis gates had not been raised behind him, and a mob of at least 400 men stormed the castle. The men-at-arms guarding the Tower put up no resistance, and the peasants shook their hands as brothers and stroked their beards in a friendly fashion ...

Perhaps the guards saw this as rather threatening behaviour!

The rebels separated into gangs and ran through the Tower searching for 'traitors'. As Froissart described, they invaded the royal apartments and behaved with little restraint, several asking 'the king's mother ... to kiss them'. The Princess Joan, known as the 'Fair Maid of Kent' was famous as a beauty. Terrified by such familiarity, the lady fainted and was carried away

to safety by her servants. Still unchallenged, the hunters drew closer to their intended victim, the Archbishop of Canterbury. Simon Sudbury, was also the King's Chancellor, and was loathed by the rebels. He had attempted an earlier escape by river but was forced to retreat to the Tower. Realising that there was little hope of escaping, he chose to spend his final hours of life preparing for an untimely death. Caught praying in the chapel, the Archbishop was dragged out of the castle and on to Tower Hill. There he was beheaded on a log of wood. It took the headsman eight strokes before the 'traitor's' head could be impaled on a spike and mounted over the gate of London Bridge.

The King later agreed to the rebels' radical demands for equality. Nevertheless, the tense situation quickly degenerated and their leader Wat Tyler was killed in the confusion. Showing remarkable courage, the teenage monarch rode forward and shouted 'You shall have no captain but me!' The rebels believed their demands would be met by their new champion and dispersed.

Richard's youthful valour had triumphed over the Tower's failure to protect his household. It would be a very different story 18 years later, when he returned as its prisoner, before losing his crown to the future Henry IV.

Main picture: The leader of the Peasants' Revolt, Wat Tyler, is slain in front of Richard II.

Above: The unfortunate Archbishop Simon Sudbury was killed during the revolt.

The Menagerie

For six hundred years, the Tower of London's most exotic prisoners were animals, as Chief Curator Lucy Worsley reveals.

The Tower's Menagerie began when medieval kings exchanged rare and strange animals as gifts. In the 13th century the Holy Roman Emperor Frederick II gave Henry III of England three real leopards ('sleek as greyhounds') in compliment to the three leopards on Henry's shield. Although described as leopards, these animals were probably lions and are the ancestors of the three lions that still appear on the England football team's shirts today.

The lions were joined at the Tower by a 'white bear' – probably a polar bear – given by the King of Norway in 1252. This bear was allowed to swim in the Thames, at the end of a long leash, to catch fish. In 1255, the King of France sent 'the only elephant ever seen in England', and 'people flocked together to see the novel sight'. By Edward II's reign, the 'Keeper of the King's Lions and Leopards' earned a regular wage.

Today you walk right over the site of the original Menagerie as you enter the Tower by the western gate. From at least the reign of Edward III, this was located in the Lion Tower, part of a barbican (the outer defence of the castle), all of which is now lost. In the early 17th century, James I had the lions' dens refurbished. Visitors could look down into a semi-circular yard lined with dens and see the 'great cisterne … for the Lyons to drinke and washe themselfes in'. James himself particularly enjoyed seeing the lions being baited by dogs.

Many of the lions and other animals did not survive long in their cramped conditions. An ostrich died in 1781 because visitors, wrongly believing it could digest iron, fed it more than 80 nails!

Some members of the Menagerie, 1210-1834

1210	1252	1255	1592	1599	1661	1697	1698	1704
first lions recorded at the Tower of London	a 'white bear' from Norway	an African elephant	a 'lean, ugly wolf'	six lions and lionesses, two of them 'over 100 years old'	two eagles	a hyena, 'a beast never seen in England before'	two 'pretty looking hell-cats'	'two Swedish Owls, of a great Bigness, called Hopkins'

The 'Extraordinary and fatal combat' between a lion, a tiger and a tigress at the Tower Menagerie in December 1830.

Although unlikely to be fatal, a bite from a famous Tower raven is to be avoided!

The keepers misguidedly gave the Tower's second elephant (a gift from the King of Spain in 1623) a gallon of wine a day to drink. Yet some of the animals had their revenge. A female leopard would seize umbrellas, parasols, muffs and hats from visitors with 'the greatest quickness' before 'tearing them into pieces', and the 'school of monkeys' was disbanded when one of its members 'tore a boy's leg'. In 1686, Mary Jenkinson died after an encounter with one of the lions. She tried to stroke him, he pounced, and her death followed on from the botched amputation of her mauled arm.

The end of the Menagerie came in the 1830s, just when it had swollen to its greatest size. Because they were expensive, occasionally dangerous and a nuisance to the garrison, the animals were dispersed, some of them going to the new zoo in Regent's Park and others going to tour America with a travelling exhibition.

As well as being pieces of living heraldry given by one king to another, the Tower animals gave thousands of people their first glimpse of the exotic beasts they could otherwise only have seen in books.

The ravens

Legend says that the kingdom and the Tower will fall if the six resident ravens ever leave the fortress. It was Charles II, according to the stories, who first insisted that the ravens of the Tower be protected. This was against the wishes of his astronomer, John Flamsteed, who complained that the ravens impeded the business of his observatory in the White Tower.

The kingdom did not in fact fall when the ravens were temporarily absent during the disruption of the Second World War, but it seems foolish to take chances. Today the Tower's seven ravens (one spare) are looked after very carefully by the Ravenmaster. They eat 170g (6oz) of raw meat a day, plus bird biscuits soaked in blood. They enjoy an egg once a week, the occasional rabbit (complete with fur) and scraps of fried bread.

Despite the painless clipping of one wing, some ravens do in fact go absent without leave and others have had to be sacked. Raven George was dismissed for eating television aerials and Grog was last seen outside an East End pub.

1741	1753	1794	1799	1821	1826	1830	1834
the lions Marco and Phillis, and their son Nero; a panther named Jenny	an ostrich	'Miss Fanny Howe', a lioness	a School of Monkeys	a grizzly bear called 'Old Martin'	a 'remarkably beautiful' ocelot	a pig-faced baboon and an alligator	a 'large and furious' wolf

The Tower and the City

Ever since its foundation the Tower has had a changing and uneasy relationship with the city on whose edge it stands, says Curator Sebastian Edwards.

The Tower was first and foremost a symbol of royal power in the City and in troubled times a refuge for the king and leaders. Although created to keep the enemy out, the Tower could only survive through commerce with the outside world and one of its first major expansions was the creation of the wharf to allow kings and merchants alike to unload goods from the river.

In the 14th century, Edward III extended the old quay next to the Lion Tower to meet the demand for military supplies during the Hundred Years' War with France. The final expansion to the east was supervised by Geoffrey Chaucer, the poet, who was also Clerk of Works at the Tower.

In the 15th century, cannons were manufactured on the wharf and it has been associated with ordnance ever since. Still today every royal visit or celebration is greeted here with a gun salute, perhaps none noisier than James I's arrival as king in 1604 to one hundred guns on the wharf.

The greater threat to the Tower has come from the City, and not the river, so the early Tower authorities soon gained control of land beyond the moat, known as the Tower Liberty. Part of this area was Tower Hill, inextricably associated with public executions. Here, about 112 people were executed, most of them nobles or gentlemen, who were generally beheaded rather than suffering the more gruesome fate of being hanged, drawn and quartered, which took place at Tyburn. These were

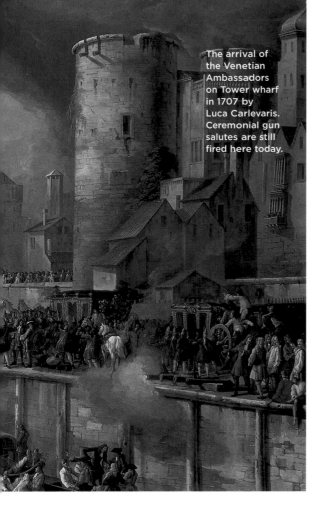

The arrival of the Venetian Ambassadors on Tower wharf in 1707 by Luca Carlevaris. Ceremonial gun salutes are still fired here today.

Strange ... but true!

The area around the Tower including Tower Hill and formerly East Smithfield, known as the Tower Liberty, is controlled by the Tower but its borders have been disputed with the City for centuries. It is marked by boundary stones and every three years on Ascension Day local children and officials walk their course and beat the stones with willow wands (below). This dates back to a 14th-century tradition that boys were actually beaten at the stones so they would remember their location.

Another curious tradition is payment of the Constable's Dues, one of several perks that the Constable of the Tower traditionally exacted from passing river traffic. Still today, whenever a Royal Naval vessel moors on the wharf the Captain must present the Constable with a barrel of rum. This is ceremoniously escorted into the Tower by the Yeoman Warders and presented to the Resident Governor. Other tariffs included any horses, oxen, pigs or sheep that fell off London Bridge.

popular events even though they were intended to subdue the rabble at times of unrest. Such was the crowd at the beheading of the Scottish rebel Lord Lovat, in 1747, that the public stands collapsed causing many injuries.

If the Tower represented royal authority, sometimes oppression even, the City of London stood for the people. When Henry III attempted to build a new fortified gate, facing the City, and it collapsed twice in as many years, it was reported that he had angered the spirit of St Thomas Becket 'who sees these buildings as an insult and danger to the Londoners; this is why he has destroyed them irreparably'. Numerous sieges of the Tower in the later Middle Ages were supported by the Mayor and the City, culminating in the Peasants' Revolt of 1381 (see page 60).

Fear of the mob – as it became known – continued for centuries and as late as 1848 the Duke of Wellington, then Constable of the Tower, built the enormous North Bastion (destroyed by a bomb in the Second World War) facing Tower Hill as part of new defences against the Chartist rioters who sought to widen the voting franchise.

Tower Hill was most recently remodelled by Stanton Williams architects in 2003. On this occasion the only crowd that shaped its design were the millions of tourists who flock to the Tower today, and the new buildings designed to welcome and entertain them.

Over the last thousand years, buildings at the Tower have withstood various sorts of attack: from a rioting mob of angry peasants, from fire, aggressive tree roots, Second World War bombs and the natural ravages of time. But the mighty Tower of London now faces challenges that none of its early builders could have anticipated; challenges that require our urgent and continuing attention, not to mention several million pounds.

Modern materials such as hard cement (instead of the traditional soft lime) are unyielding and unsympathetic to the crumbling old stones. And William the Conqueror could not have dreamed of the fortress being explored by our lovely visitors with rucksack straps, sticky fingers, ice-cream cones and felt-tipped pens!

Looking after the Tower is an ongoing responsibility, but conservation as opposed to restoration or repair, is a modern notion. In the past if a building became old and neglected, it either fell, or was torn down and a new one built. The idea that there is value in old buildings because of the stories they can tell is fairly new. The approach we take today is founded on conservation controversies that raged in the 20th century, but didn't stop the demolition of historic buildings, right up to the 1970s.

A lot of money was spent on 'repairing' or tidying up the Tower by the Victorian architect Anthony Salvin (see page 13). As part of his 'medievalisation' project he refaced the curtain walls with regular coursed stones and a cement mortar. After rain, the moisture could not evaporate through the mortar but dried through the stone, causing it to crumble.

In cold weather, as the water freezes and expands, bits of stone break off. What Salvin should have done is to have used a lime mortar, softer than the stones, which allows the wall to dry out through the mortar joints.

In the past 30 years there has been more care given to repair using traditional methods and materials. So instead of asphalting a roof we will repair using the traditional slate, tiles or lead coverings. If timber has rotted, we will replace only the decayed section and keep as much of the original in situ as possible. The same approach is used for stone and brick repairs. These repairs tend to last longer and give better value for money, too.

There is so much these buildings can still tell us that we must preserve what we can for future generations to discover.

The last battle

Historic Royal Palaces' Surveyor, Jo Thwaites, explains the ongoing fight to protect the Tower for future generations.

War on all fronts

Conservation doesn't come cheap! Just to give you an idea, these are a few of our future projects. (Oh, and VAT isn't included …)

- It cost £1.5 million to clean, repoint and repair crumbling stones on the south elevation of the White Tower, with three more elevations to go starting in spring 2008 at a total cost of around £2.5m.

- The Beauchamp, Constable and Bloody towers all need repairs to their lead roofs, plus masonry work. This vital work will start in spring 2007, at an estimated total cost of £985,000.

- We need to resurface Tower Green, starting in May 2007, at a cost of around £100,000.

To find out how you can support this essential work, please visit **www.hrp.org.uk**

'Moat wall collapses at the Tower of London! Is this the end of civilisation as we know it and will the ravens fly away?'

This was how the newspapers reported a dramatic event on a frosty morning in February 2003. However, the real story was that behind the collapsed wall (undermined by tree roots) there was a 15th-century wall made of beautifully-dressed Reigate stone, dating from the time when cannon were manufactured on the wharf. Traces of the 14th-century wharf beneath, built on the orders of the poet Geoffrey Chaucer, Clerk of Works for Richard II, were found too. A team of archaeologists discovered even more, including part of a factory where weapons were made to fight against Napoleon. We were able to record every stage of the exploration before carrying out the essential repair work, adding further to our understanding of the historical development of the Tower.

In the rucksack zone

We are delighted to welcome over two million visitors a year to the Tower, but can I make a plea on behalf of these ancient buildings: please could you remove your rucksacks? If you look carefully you'll see what we call 'the rucksack zone': the shoulder-height abrasions from the rubbing and scraping of millions of straps and buckles. Soft Reigate stone is most vulnerable and the wear and tear on the Bell Tower is one of the worst – you can see the hollowing out of the stone. Damage was so bad in the tight narrow spiral of the Bloody Tower staircase we had to make a metal protector shield for the wall. In some areas the damage is so bad the stone has to be replaced, or walls really will come tumbling down!

Four more palaces to explore; hundreds of stories to discover

Hampton Court Palace

Explore Henry VIII's magnificent palace, then stroll through the elegant Baroque apartments and glorious formal gardens of William III and Mary II. Feel the heat of the vast Tudor Kitchens and the eerie chill of the Haunted Gallery, before you disappear into the fiendish Maze ...

Recorded information: 0870 752 7777

Banqueting House

Walk in the footsteps of a dazzling company of courtiers who once danced, drank and partied beneath Rubens's magnificent painted ceiling. This revolutionary building was created for court entertainments, but is probably most famous for the execution of Charles I in 1649. Spare him a thought as you gaze up at this ravishing painting – one of his last sights on earth ...

Recorded information: 0870 751 5187

Kew Palace & Queen Charlotte's Cottage

Step into this tiny doll's house of a palace and experience the joys and sorrows of King George III and his family through a radio play and displays of fascinating personal artefacts. Stroll to Queen Charlotte's Cottage, built in 1770, where the royal family enjoyed picnics and peace in a tranquil corner of Kew Gardens.

Open April – October. Entry to Kew Gardens is required to visit Kew Palace and Queen Charlotte's Cottage.

Recorded information: 0870 751 5174

Kensington Palace

Marvel at the stunning collection of English court dress at this stylish palace, a unique archive of royal fashion from the 18th century to the present day – including several evening dresses worn by Diana, Princess of Wales. Explore the magnificent State Apartments and take tea in the Orangery designed for Queen Anne in 1704.

Recorded information: 0870 751 5170

We offer an exciting programme of events and exhibitions throughout the year. For more information and details on tickets and how to find us, please visit www.hrp.org.uk

Supporting us

Historic Royal Palaces is the independent charity that looks after the Tower of London, Hampton Court Palace, the Banqueting House, Kensington Palace and Kew Palace. We help everyone explore the story of how monarchs and people have shaped society in some of the greatest palaces ever built.

We receive no funding from the Government or the Crown so we depend on the support of our visitors, members, donors, volunteers and sponsors.

Can you help?

We hope that you have thoroughly enjoyed your visit to the Tower of London and have discovered more about the conservation of this ancient building. Our work goes on; funds will always be needed to protect and maintain the Tower. Any donation that you can spare means this valuable work can continue. Please call the Development Department on **0845 389 3003** for more information, or email **development@hrp.org.uk**. Thank you.

Join us!

Joining Historic Royal Palaces is the perfect way to explore the inside stories of five extraordinary places that helped define our nation's history. What's more, you'll save money and contribute to the important work of conserving the palaces at the same time.

It's amazing value; membership of Historic Royal Palaces means you have the freedom to visit the Tower of London, Hampton Court Palace, the Banqueting House, Kensington Palace and Kew Palace (open April – October) as often as you like. Membership also means you don't have to queue – simply walk in to see, experience and understand what made us who we are. Other benefits include exclusive members-only events, behind-the-scenes tours and great discounts in our shops and online.

Make a present of the past

Step through the doors of a royal palace and you are surrounded by stories of strategy, intrigue, ambition, romance, devotion and disaster. What more inspiring gift could there be than a Historic Royal Palaces Membership for someone who shares your love of history, amazing buildings, their beautiful contents and gorgeous gardens?

To enquire about becoming a member of Historic Royal Palaces and for more information on the range of benefits you receive please visit **www.hrp.org.uk** or call **0870 751 5174**.

Further reading

The Armour & Arms of Henry VIII
Thom Richardson
The Royal Armouries, 2002

The Crown Jewels: Official Guidebook
Anna Keay
Historic Royal Palaces, 2002

The Elizabethan Tower of London:
The Haiward and Gascoyne plan of 1597
Anna Keay
London Topographical Society with
Historic Royal Palaces, 2001

Prisoners of the Tower: The Tower of London
as a state prison, 1100-1941
Jeremy Ashbee et al.
Historic Royal Palaces, 2004

The private life of palaces
Julian Humphrys
Historic Royal Palaces, 2006

The Royal Menagerie at the Tower of London
Geoffrey Parnell
The Royal Armouries, 1999

Tales from the Tower
Fiona Jerome
Think Books with Historic Royal Palaces, 2006

The Tower Menagerie
Daniel Hahn
Simon & Schuster, 2003

The Tower of London: A 2000-year History
Ivan Lapper and Geoffrey Parnell
Osprey Publishing, 2000

The Tower of London: Its Buildings and Institutions
John Charlton (ed)
HMSO, 1977

The Tower of London Moat: Archaeological
Excavations, 1995-9
Graham Keevill
Oxford Archaeology with Historic Royal Palaces, 2004

The Tower of London: The Official Illustrated History
Edward Impey and Geoffrey Parnell
Merrell Publishers, 2000

Tower Power: Tales from the Tower of London
Elizabeth Newbery
Historic Royal Palaces, 2004

The White Tower
Edward Impey (ed)
Yale University Press, 2008

Visit our online store for our full range of books and beautiful gifts inspired by centuries of stories from five amazing palaces:
www.historicroyalpalaces.com

From *Tower Power: Tales from the Tower of London*

House of Normandy	William I	1066-1087
	William II	1087-1100
	Henry I	1100-1135
	Stephen	1135-1154
House of Plantagenet	Henry II	1154-1189
	Richard I	1189-1199
	John	1199-1216
	Henry III	1216-1272
	Edward I	1272-1307
	Edward II	1307-1327
	Edward III	1327-1377
	Richard II	1377-1399
	Henry IV	1399-1413
	Henry V	1413-1422
	Henry VI	1422-1461
		1470-1471
	Edward IV	1461-1470
		1471-1483
	Edward V	1483
	Richard III	1483-1485
House of Tudor	Henry VII	1485-1509
	Henry VIII	1509-1547
	Edward VI	1547-1553
	Mary I	1553-1558
	Elizabeth I	1558-1603
House of Stuart	James I	1603-1625
	Charles I	1625-1649
	The Commonwealth	1649-1660
	Charles II	1660-1685
	James II	1685-1688
	William III	1689-1702
	& Mary II	1689-1694
	Anne*	1702-1714
House of Hanover	George I	1714-1727
	George II	1727-1760
	George III	1760-1820
	George IV	1820-1830
	William IV	1830-1837
	Victoria	1837-1901
House of Saxe-Coburg-Gotha	Edward VII	1901-1910
House of Windsor	George V	1910-1936
	Edward VIII	1936
	George VI	1936-1952
	Elizabeth II	Succeeded 1952

* First monarch of Great Britain

Kings & queens of England

Glossary

Arsenal:
An establishment for the manufacture and storage of arms and ammunition.

Barbican:
An outer defence protecting the entrance to a castle.

Bastion:
A structure projecting outwards from the main walls of a fortress, from which the castle is defended.

Curtain wall:
A wall enclosing a castle, or one of its parts.

Keep:
A relatively large tower within a castle, usually intended as a residence and its innermost stronghold.

Loop:
A narrow vertical slit in a defensive wall, from which bows and guns could be fired.

Mural towers:
Towers set between stretches of wall.

Ordnance:
Artillery supplies.

Portcullis:
A heavy iron or wooden grating lowered vertically as a defensive barrier at the entrance of a gatehouse.

Historic Royal PALACES

Historic Royal Palaces is the independent charity that looks after the Tower of London, Hampton Court Palace, the Banqueting House, Kensington Palace and Kew Palace. We help everyone explore the story of how monarchs and people have shaped society, in some of the greatest palaces ever built.

We receive no funding from the Government or the Crown, so we depend on the support of our visitors, members, donors, volunteers and sponsors.

Acknowledgements

Published by Historic Royal Palaces
Hampton Court Palace
Surrey
KT8 9AU

© Historic Royal Palaces, 2007

All rights reserved. No part of this publication may be reproduced or transmitted in any form or by any means electronic or mechanical, including photocopying, recording or any information storage and retrieval system, without permission in writing from the publisher.

ISBN 978-1-873993-01-9

Written by Brett Dolman (tours 3 & 4), Susan Holmes (History), Edward Impey (tour 5) and Jane Spooner (tours 1, 2 & 6). Additional research by Sally Dixon-Smith.

Edited by Sarah Kilby and Clare Murphy
Designed by www.brandremedy.com
Principal photography by Nick Guttridge
Illustration inside front cover by Stephen Conlin
Illustrations pages 8, 27b, 57 by Ivan Lapper
Illustration page 15 by Edward Impey
Illustrations pages 46-7, 70 by Tim Archbold
Illustrations inside back cover by Robin Wyatt
Printed by Inkon Printers Limited

Illustrations
Unless otherwise indicated, all illustrations are © Historic Royal Palaces.

Abbreviations: b = bottom, c = centre, l = left, r = right, t = top

The Board of Trustees of the Armouries: pages 19t, 26l, 37t, 52, 53, 54-5, 59b, 62, 63bl, 63br; Bayerische Staatsgemäldesammlungen: pages 64-5; The Bridgeman Art Library, London: pages 7 (The City of Bayeux, Musée de la Tapisserie, Bayeux, France), 10t (Centrale Bibliotheek van de Universiteit, Ghent, Belgium), 39 (Roy Miles Fine Paintings), 60 (© The British Library, Roy 18 E 1 f.175), 63tl (Guildhall Library, City of London); By permission of the British Library: pages 9l (Cott Claud DII f.113), 28-9 (Royal MS 14 EIV f.244v), 31 (Cott MS Vit AXIII f.6v), 35b (Harl 4380 f.181v), 49 (Royal MS 16 F ii f.73); © Copyright The Trustees of The British Museum: page 12; City of London, London Metropolitan Archives: page 19b; Crown copyright: page 9r; Ministry of Defence Art Collection, London: page 13; Getty Images – Hulton Archive: page 65; © Historic Royal Palaces/ newsteam.co.uk: page 25t; The Master and Fellows of Magdalene College, Cambridge: page 45; Courtesy of the Museum of London: pages 27t, 61 (St Gregory, Sudbury. Not on public display; viewing by prior appointment); © The National Gallery, London: pages 32-3; National Portrait Gallery, London: pages 26r, 34tr; Reproduced by kind permission of His Grace The Duke of Norfolk, Arundel Castle: page 36r; © HM Queen Elizabeth II 2001: pages 5l, 42, 43, 44; The Royal Collection © 2007 Her Majesty Queen Elizabeth II: page 11t; Sotheby's Picture Library, London: page 10b; Courtesy of Universal Studios Licensing LLLP (photograph: British Film Institute): page 38.

The exhibition *Crowns and Diamonds: the making of the Crown Jewels* has been made possible by the generosity of De Beers. Their contribution is gratefully acknowledged.

Historic Royal Palaces is a registered charity (no. 1068852).

www.hrp.org.uk